CW00673259

Short Guides to Records

FIRST SERIES — GUIDES 1 - 24

Published by The Historical Association

This edition has been edited by Dr K M Thompson.

The Historical Association, founded in 1906, brings together people who share an interest in, and love for, the past. It aims to further the study and teaching of history at all levels: teacher and student, amateur and professional. This is one of over 100 publications available at very preferential rates to members. Membership also includes discount on Journals and access to courses, conferences, tours and regional and local activities. Full details are available from The Secretary, The Historical Association, 59a Kennington Park Road, London, SE11 4JH, telephone: 071 735 3901, fax: 071 582 4989.

The publication of a book by the Historical Association does not necessarily imply the Association's approval of the opinions expressed in it.

© The Historical Association, 1994

Preparation and layout by Madeline Stiles and Tracey Richardson, The Historical Association.

ISBN 0 85278 347 7

Published by The Historical Association, 59a Kennington Park Road, London, SE11 4JH and printed in Great Britain by Blackmore Press, Longmead Industrial Estate, Shaftesbury, Dorset ,SP7 8PX.

Contents

Foreword

In 1990 the Local History Committee of the Historical Association, with the benefit of a grant from the Aurelius Trust, decided to produce a new series of *Short Guides to Records* to follow up the successful venture of the 1960s. The new guides would deal with a different set of records, but there remained a continuing demand for the earlier series. It was, however, unrealistic to revise a text written by some two dozen authors at the same time as producing the new set of guides. The current volume has therefore been reset, in order to bring it in line with the new series, but has not otherwise been altered. To increase its usefulness, a new introductory chapter and bibliography have been added. It is to be hoped that, in this new edition, the guides may continue to help local historians as they tackle new record sources.

No attempt has been made to bring the volume in line with the changed and changing world of local government organisation. The reader will still find a reference to the London County Council, and the original publication predated the GLC and the Metropolitan counties. But in a world in which some of the historic County Councils themselves may disappear and a potential threat exists to the system of county record offices so painstakingly and successfully built up in recent decades, and which has had a transforming influence on the study of history and on the local historian, it would perhaps be rash to attempt such a revision. However, an explanatory outline of the changes in record offices since the first edition, will be found in the preface.

We wish to record our thanks to Dr Kate Thompson for her work in editing this volume and the accompanying new series of *Short Guides to Records*, to Gordon Forster who provided the additional bibliography, to Madeline Stiles and the Headquarters staff for setting the text, and to the Local History Committee for checking the proofs.

Marilyn Palmer
Chairman, Local History Committee
of the Historical Association, 1989-1993

John Hare
Chairman, Local History Committee
of the Historical Association, 1993-

Preface

to the New Edition

Since Lionel Munby edited the first series of *Short Guides to Records* and wrote its introduction in 1972 much has happened on the local history scene. The original set of 24 titles was published between 1961 and 1971 in *History* and was only terminated as a result of a change in editorial policy.

It is not an exaggeration to say that there has been an explosion in local history activity in the last 20 years. At the academic level several universities now offer certificates, diplomas and higher degrees in the subject and at least one also runs a BA degree course. An important landmark was the publication of the report of the Committee to Review Local History (chaired by Lord Blake) in 1979 which led to the establishment of the British Association for Local History (BALH) in 1982. This new body received generous financial assistance in its first three years which enabled it to appoint a field officer, whose role was to discover the amount and type of local history activity in the country at large. David Hayns' reports are a fascinating snapshot and include detailed studies of a number of counties.

BALH also took over responsibility for *The Local Historian*, which had started life in 1952 as *The Amateur Historian*. It remains the pre-eminent academic journal and there is no slackening in the quantity and quality of material submitted to its editor. Another national publication, *Local History Magazine*, began life in 1984. The Historical Association's quarterly magazine, *The Historian*, usually contains one local history article. At the sub-national level local history titles proliferate: most counties in England and Wales have a county-wide journal, there are regional publications and in addition hundreds of titles covering smaller areas. These vary in sophistication, quality and frequency and many have benefited from the availability of relatively cheap desktop publishing packages.

Another new initiative which has spread across the country like wildfire is the local history fair. These first appeared in the early 1980s and have since been held all over the British Isles. They range from one-county affairs held for a day to regional activities lasting for a weekend. They bring together local historians and others interested in the past, and usually contain a mixture of historical re-enactments, displays by local societies and bookstalls. The more popular events, such as the Essex fairs, attract thousands of people and even in the winter there is at least one local history event held somewhere in the country every week. The British Association for Local History published a guide in 1989, *Running a local history fair* by Vic Gray and Bill Liddell.

At the grass-roots level interest in local history has mushroomed. The Historical Association has long had a network of local branches, some of which have been very active in research and publication. Many talks to HA branches have a local history theme. There are hundreds of local history societies, varying in size and activity, as well as specialist societies. Most counties in

England and Wales have an 'umbrella' organisation which co-ordinates activity in its area. Much of the increased interest in local history has stemmed from the family history 'boom'. Many adults were attracted to history through a desire to know more about their own antecedents and it is a logical next step to wish to understand the kind of lives lived by their ancestors. Many family historians have 'moved on' to local history and some very worthy research has resulted.

Both family and local historians have undertaken much research that has helped others. The family historians in particular have been very active in producing indexes to popular records such as the census returns and poor law papers, which has the additional benefit of reducing wear and tear on original records. All of this activity has put pressure on record offices which has caused short-term problems. However most archivists welcome this increased use as evidence of the value placed on their services by a growing number of local tax payers. A number of 'Friends of Record Offices' have been formed from the Public Record Office downwards; at the national level the National Council on Archives brings together professional bodies, such as the Society of Archivists and the Association of County Archivists, and user groups, such as the Federation of Family History Societies, the British Association for Local History and the Historical Association. Public support for record offices has been impressive and it is clear that attempts to curtail archive services will meet with very vocal resistance.

The efforts of archivists and others have introduced local historians to previously unknown sources for research. It is now much easier to get information on the whereabouts of different types of records and the second series of *Short Guides* will help in this process. The number of instructional books for local historians has blossomed since Lionel Munby wrote his introduction to the first series and a new bibliography accompanies the second series. There are a number of specialist publishers, such as Phillimore and Alan Sutton, who sell textbooks and studies of individual places and subjects for the whole country. Other publishers specialise in a particular region or subject and many of the major firms now include some local history titles in their lists. In addition the Historical Association, the British Association for Local History and the Federation of Family History Societies all produce short pamphlets and occasionally longer works on the subject. BALH for example has published two educational books for schools: *The Late Victorian Town* and *The Union Workhouse,* with the help of the Gulbenkian Foundation.

CHANGES IN RECORD OFFICES

Since the first series of *Short Guides* was published there have been considerable changes in the record office network: several county record offices have moved to new or converted accommodation and the structure has altered in some areas. The most obvious change occurred as a result of the abolition of the Greater London Council and Metropolitan County Councils in

1986. The current review of shire counties may well result in further changes.

Most London boroughs have an archives department, often as part of the library service. The London-wide record office is the Greater London Record Office (GLRO), 40 Northampton Road, London, EC1R 0HB (tel 071 332 3820). It is administered by the Corporation of London in addition to its two other record offices — the Guildhall Library and the Corporation of London Records [sic] Office.

In the Metropolitan areas there are joint services in Greater Manchester, Tyne and Wear and West Yorkshire. In Merseyside there are record offices in three of the four Metropolitan districts (the exception being Sefton) and the Merseyside Record Office keeps the records of the former Merseyside County Council and the residuary body, together with other 'cross-district' records such as those for nonconformist denominations, charities and hospitals. South Yorkshire has four independent record offices but joint arrangements for conservation and the records of the former Council Council. (There was never a county-wide service for the former West Midlands County Council.)

For up to date information on all publicly funded record offices in the United Kingdom the best guide is *Record Repositories in Great Britain* (9th edition revised, 1992) or consult the Royal Commission on Historical Manuscripts, Quality House, Quality Court, Chancery Lane, London, WC2A 1HP (tel 071 242 1198).

Dr K M Thompson

Selected Additional Bibliography

Since the publication of the *Short Guides* and of Mr L M Munby's 'Introduction' several general works on archives, sources and methods, as well as numerous guides to specific sources, have been published. The most useful and accessible of these publications are listed below; this list should be used in conjunction with the original bibliographical references given in the "Introduction" or appended to each of the *Short Guides*.

Directories and General Guides to Archive Collections

(i) Directories

Record repositories in Great Britain: a geographical survey (9th edn, HMSO, 1991)

Foster, J and Sheppard, J, *British Archives: a guide to archive resources in the United Kingdom* (2nd edn, Macmillan, 1989)

Williams, M I, *A Directory of Rare Book and Special Collections in the United Kingdom and the Republic of Ireland* (Library Association, 1985)

(ii) General Guides to Archives

The National Inventory of Documentary Sources in the United Kingdom: published and unpublished finding aids to archives and manuscript collections, reproduced on microfiche, with an index [in progress]

Royal Commission on Historical Manuscripts, publications include:

Guide to the Reports 1870-1957: Index of Places; Index of Persons (7 vols, HMSO, 1914-66)

Guide to the Location of Collections described in the Reports and Calendars Series, 1870-1980 (HMSO, 1982)

Guides to Sources for British History (HMSO): several volumes (apart from

 © The Historical Association, 1994

the *Guide to the Location of Collections)*, including: papers of churchmen, 1780-1940; politicians, 1782-1900; business and industry, 1760-1914

Surveys of Historical Manuscripts in the United Kingdom (HMSO, 1989)

Barley, M W, *A Guide to British Topographical Collections* (Council for British Archaeology, 1974)

Public Record Office: Current Guide, 1992 edn on microfiche

Maps and Plans in the Public Record Office (HMSO, 1967)

British Library:

> **Skeat, T C,** *The Catalogues of the Manuscript Collections in the British Museum* (1962)
>
> **Nickson, M A E,** *The British Library: Guide to the catalogues and indexes of the Department of Manuscripts* (1978)
>
> *Catalogue of the Newspaper Library, Colindale* (1975)
>
> *Catalogue of the manuscript maps, charts and plans, and of the topographical drawings* (1962)
>
> *Catalogue of the printed maps, charts and plans* (1964)

Printed historical records: **Mullins E L C,** *Texts and Calendars: an analytical guide to serial publications* [to 1982] (Royal Historical Society Guides and Handbooks, nos. 7 and 12, 2 vols. 1958, 1983)

Guides to Sources and Methods

(i)   Sources: General

> **Bagley, J J,** *Historical Interpretation: sources of English history* (2 vols, Penguin, 1972)
>
> **Elton, G R,** *England 1200-1640* (Cambridge University Press, 1969)
>
> **Lambert, S,** *Bills and Acts* (Cambridge University Press, 1971)
>
> **Macfarlane, A,** *A Guide to English Historical Records* (Cambridge University Press, 1983)

Morton, A and Donaldson, G, *British National Archives and the Local Historian* (H.A. Helps series, no.88, n.d.)

Riden, P J, *Record Sources for Local History* (Batsford, 1987)

Stephens, W B, *Sources for English Local History* (2nd edn, Cambridge University Press, 1981)

(ii) Methods and the Use of Sources: General

Dymond, D P, *Writing Local History* (Phillimore, 1988)

Elton, G R, *The Practice of History* (Collins/Fontana, 1972)

Hoskins, W G, *Local History in England* (3rd edn, Longman, 1984)

Riden, P J, *Local History* (Batsford, 1983)

Rogers, A, (comp) *Approaches to Local History* (Longman, 1977)

Tiller, K, *English Local History* (Alan Sutton, 1992)

(iii) Guides to Specific Sources

Alcock, N W, *Old Title Deeds* (Phillimore, 1986)

Alldridge, N J, (ed.) *The Hearth Tax* (Humberside College [now University], 1983)

Beckett, J V, *Local Taxation* (Phillimore, 1980)

Beresford, M W, *Lay Subsidies and Poll Taxes* (Phillimore, 1963)

Bettey, J H, *Church and Parish: a guide for local historians* (Batsford, 1987)

Camp, A J, *Wills and their Whereabouts* (privately published, 1974)

Dibben, A A, *Title Deeds* (Historical Association, Helps series, no.72, 1971)

Edwards, P, *Farming: Sources for Local Historians* (Batsford, 1991)

Edwards, P, *Rural Life: Guide to Local Records* (Batsford, 1993)

 © The Historical Association, 1994

Elton, E A, Harrison, B and Wark, K R, *Researching the Country House* (Batsford, 1992)

Emmison, F G and Gray, I, *County Records* (H.A. Helps series, no.62, 1973, 1987)

Evans, E J, *Tithes, Maps, Apportionments and the 1836 Act* (Phillimore, for the British Association for Local History, 1993)

Gibson, J S W, *Wills and Where to Find Them* (Phillimore, 1974)

Gibson, J S W, *Local Newspapers 1750-1920: a select location list* (Federation of Family History Societies, 1987)

Harley ,J B and Phillips, C W, *The Historian's Guide to Ordnance Survey Maps* (Standing Conference for Local History, 1964)

Harley, J B, *Maps for the Local Historian* (Standing Conference for Local History, 1972)

Harvey, P D A, *Manorial Records* (British Records Association, 1984)

Harvey, J H, *Sources for the History of Houses* (British Records Association, 1974)

Hey, D G, *Family History and Local History in England* (Longman, 1987)

Hey, D G, *The Oxford Guide to Family History* (Oxford University Press, 1993)

Hindle, B P, *Maps for Local History* (Batsford, 1988)

Kain, R J P and Prince, H C, *The Tithe Surveys of England and Wales* (Cambridge University Press, 1985)

Macfarlane, A, *Reconstructing Historical Communities* (Cambridge University Press, 1977)

Mullett, M, *Sources for the History of English Nonconformity 1660-1830* (British Records Association, 1991)

Murphy, M, *Newspapers and Local History* (Phillimore, 1991)

Oliver, G, *Photographs and Local History* (Batsford, 1990)

Owen, D M, *Bishops' Registers* (Historical Association, Helps series, no. 89, 1982)

Porter, S, *Exploring Urban History* (Batsford, 1990)

Public Record Office Handbooks:

Tracing your Ancestors (HMSO, 1981)
Making Sense of the Census (HMSO, 1989)

Purvis, J S, *An Introduction to Ecclesiastical Records* (St Anthony's Press, 1953)

Shaw, G and Tipper, A, *British Directories* (Leicester University Press, 1988)

Smith, D M, *Guide to Bishops' Registers of England and Wales* (Royal Historical Society Guides and Handbooks, no. 11, 1981)

Stephens, W B and Unwin, R W, *Materials for the Local and Regional Study of Schooling 1700-1900* (British Records Association, 1987)

Storey, R L and Beresford, M W, *Introduction to Wills and the Unprinted Census Returns of 1841, 1851, 1861* (Phillimore, 1966)

Stuart, D, *Manorial Records* (Phillimore, 1992)

The Times Tercentenary Handlist of English and Welsh Newspapers, Magazines and Reviews (*The Times*, 1920)

Toase, C A, *Bibliography of British Newspapers* (Library Association, 1975 — in progress)

Turner, M and Mills, D (eds.) *Land and Property: the English Land Tax 1692- 1832* (Alan Sutton, 1986)

Ward, W R, *The Administration of the Window and Assessed Taxes 1696-1798* (Phillimore, 1963)

West, J, *Town Records* (Phillimore, 1984)

Wrigley, E A (ed.) *English Historical Demography* (Weidenfeld & Nicolson, 1966)

© The Historical Association, 1994

Reference

Friar, S, *The Batsford Companion to Local History* (Batsford, 1991)

Elton, G R and others (eds.) *Royal Historical Society Annual Bibliography of British and Irish History, Publications of 1975-* (1976 — in progress) Hall, A T, *Local History Handlist* (Historical Association, Helps series, no.69, n.d.)

Horn, J M, *History Theses, 1971-80* (Institute of Historical Research, University of London, 1984)

Jacobs, P M, *History Theses, 1901-70* (Institute of Historical Research, University of London, 1976)

Milne, A T and others (eds.) *Writings on British History, 1901-33; 1934-45; 1946-57; 1958-74* (27 vols, variously published, 1937-86)

Mullins, E L C (ed.) *Guide to the Historical and Archaeological Publications of Societies in England and Wales, 1901-33* (Athlone Press, 1968)

Youngs, F A, *Guide to the Local Administrative Units of England* (Royal Historical Society Guides and Handbooks, nos. 10, 17, 2 vols, 1979, 1991)

G C F Forster

Introduction

The twenty-four *Short Guides to Records* which are bound together in this book were printed in *History* between 1961 and 1971 and were also issued as separate publications. They were sponsored by the Historical Association's Local History Committee and intended as brief introductions for the student to whom individual classes of records were new. The series grew without any preconceived plan, except that a balance between records from different periods was aimed at and that the records chosen were those likely to be of more than specialist interest and of use to the student of a locality rather than to the historian of the nation. The very varied records covered are to be found in many different types of Record Offices, as the sections in each *Short Guide* on Location make clear. Perhaps the biggest problem which faces any one who is beginning to work on the history of a locality is to know what original material to look for and where to look for it. Two books may be recommended as guides to the whole field F G Emmison's *Archives and Local History* (Methuen, 112 + XVI pp. 32 ill., 1966) and Robert Douch's *Local History and the Teacher* (Routledge, 214 + IX pp. 1967). This introduction will, it is hoped, help the beginner one step up the ladder towards the many refined aids which are now available.

There are two things, which it is helpful to know, about records: where they came from, that is who produced them; and where they are kept. The oldest records are those produced by public institutions; the church and the government, central and local. Mrs Dorothy Owen's *The Records of the Established Church in England* (British Record Association, 64 pp. 1970) is the best introduction to church records; it tells you what they are, why they are and where they are. Dr Kathleen Major's *A Handlist of the Records of the Bishop of Lincoln and of the Archdeacons of Lincoln and Stow* (OUP, 122 + XV pp. 1953) reveals what may be found in one diocese. Mrs Owen does not deal with parochial records. W E Tate's work, *The Parish Chest* (CUP, 346 + XI pp. 1st edition 1946. 3rd edition 1969) 'a study of the Records of Parochial Administration in England', fills the gap. It is a most idiosyncratic classic, typical of its author, excellent bedside browsing but also useful for reference. The Society of Genealogists (37 Harrington Gardens, London SW7) is producing a twelve volume *National Index of Parish Registers* (Phillimore), which describes Anglican, Nonconformist, Roman Catholic and Jewish record sources. The first two volumes published contain a surprisingly wide range of general information about record sources and their use; the remainder are detailed guides to the relevant records of particular areas. A useful pamphlet is *How to write a local history of Methodism* by Wesley F Swift, revised by Thomas Shaw (Wesley Historical Society, 19 pp. 1964). Church records are to be found in Lambeth Palace Library, London SE1, in Dioceses, many of which have made the appropriate County Record Office their depository, and in Parish Churches and Chapels; the majority of parish records of all kinds are

Introduction

increasingly to be found in County Record Offices. Nonconformist records may be in the keeping of their central body, as for example the Society of Friends, Friends' House, Euston Road, London NW1, which has many fascinating early Quaker records, or Dr Williams' Library, 14 Gordon Square, London WC1, which is a general Nonconformist library and records depository. Most of the older Nonconformist registers are now in the Public Record Office. The *National Index* volumes contain full lists of these central bodies and excellent bibliographies.

Most central Government records end up in the Public Record Office, Chancery Lane, London WC2A 1LR. This probably contains the most splendid and diverse series of records of any record office in the world, but it is an extremely difficult place for the beginner to work in. Its buildings are Victorian (though a new structure is now promised at Kew), the pressure on its space is overwhelming, and a sequence of niggardly Governments has hardly increased its administrative staff since the beginning of the century. It stands as a historic example of the British habit of muddling through by providing inadequate resources for its public servants and expecting their loyalty to work miracles. The collections in the Public Record Office are so vast, and the working conditions for researchers at the moment so cramped and difficult, that it is imperative to make full use of the three volume *Guide to the Contents of the Public Record Office* (HMSO, vol. 1.Legal Records, 249 + IV pp., 1963; vol 2, State Papers and Departmental Records, 41 0 + VII pp., 1963; vol.3, Documents Transferred, 1960-66, 191 + VII pp., 1968) before visiting, and to allow plenty of time for each visit. From the printed *Guide* the student needs to go to many calendars and lists on the shelves of the Public Record Office, and constantly to seek advice from the staff on duty in the Search Rooms.

A great deal of central record material emanated from Parliament. Much of this has been printed, notably the vast series of nineteenth and twentieth century sessional papers. The best way to approach this is with the help of W R Powell's *Local History from Blue Books* (Historical Association, 43 pp., 1962). Most of the earlier House of Commons Records were lost in the fire of 1834 which destroyed the Palace of Westminster, but subsequent Commons records together with all the other surviving records of Parliament are preserved in the House of Lords Record Office in the Victoria Tower. This office has been transformed since the Second World War into a model of a Record Office under the care of Maurice Bond, OBE. His *Guide to the Records of Parliament* (HMSO, 352 + X pp., 17 ill. 1971) provides an introduction to all the groups available at Westminster; the records between 1497 and 1714 have been calendared in volumes published by the Historical Manuscripts Commission and then as House of Lords Papers.

Local government records are the responsibility of the Clerk. In nearly every county and some cities and towns there is now an office in which these records are kept and, in most cases, made available for students to use. *Record Repositories in Great Britain* (HMSO, 60 + XII pp. 1971), prepared jointly by the Historical Manuscripts Commission and the British Records Association, gives essential information about these record offices. *County Records* (Historical Association, 32 pp. revised 1967) gives details of County Record Offices. Many counties now publish their own guides, from which a clear picture of what local government records are available can be obtained. Part I of the *Guide to the Essex Record Office* by F.G Emmison (Essex County Council, Chelmsford. 85 + VII pp. 1969) covers the county's 'quarter sessions, boroughs, other official and ecclesiastical archives'. Part I of the *Guide to the Hertfordshire Record Office* edited by William Le Hardy (Herts. County Council, County Hall, Hertford. 283 + XIX pp. 1961) describes 'Quarter Sessions and other records in the custody of the officials of the county'; it is fuller than the Essex guide. Both give information about the general context of law and custom within which local institutions worked and produced their records. Shorter guides have been produced by counties as different as Caernarvonshire (45 + XV pp. 1952), London (Part I Records of the predecessors of the LCC 69 pp. 1962), and Wiltshire (Part II 131 + IX pp. 1961). Gloucestershire, as an example, has published *A short handlist of the contents of Gloucestershire Records Office* (13 pp. 1968). A great deal of information can be obtained from the annual reports of some archivists, where these give details of accessions of documents during the year in question. Lincolnshire's *Archivists' Reports* are models in this connection and, not surprisingly, a consolidated index has been published — *Index to Archivists' Reports 1948-58* (Lincolnshire Archives Committee, The Castle, Lincoln. 170 pp. 1961). Lancashire Record Office (Sessions House, Lancaster Road, Preston) annual reports combine a simple list of accessions with brief articles on particularly interesting ones. In many towns the effective local record office may be the library. Philip Hepworth's *Archives and Manuscripts in Libraries* (The Library Association, Chaucer House, Malet Place, London W C I.70 pp. second edition 1964. Library Association Pamphlet No. 18) has a great deal of information about libraries with documents in their keeping and lists published catalogues and guides to them.

Quarter Sessions records have been central to the activity of local government. Those in some counties have been calendared and the study of such a calendar is an effective way of learning about local government records. Hertfordshire has the fullest set of Calendars of Quarter Sessions Records in print in ten volumes (HCC). Warwickshire has published similar calendars for the late seventeenth century in its *Warwick County Records* series (Warwickshire County Council, Shire Hall, Warwick). There is a *Guide to the Middlesex Sessions Records* (GLC Record Office, I Queen Anne's Gate Buildings, Dartmouth Street, London SWI, 98 pp. 1965). Information about which counties have published calendars of their Quarter Sessions papers can be found in John West's *Village Records* (Macmillan, 208 + XVI pp. illus. 1962).

John West's book is a useful introduction to a carefully selected number of records which the village historian needs. Many of these are privately produced. Part II of the *Guide to the Essex Record Office* (166 pp.) deals with 'Estate, Family and Business Archives, etc.' and is naturally much more

Introduction

comprehensive. What kind of document the local historian will find in any given record office is quite unpredictable. The best archivists are like squirrels: they collect all that they can get their hands on and have room for. What are called 'Unofficial Deposited Archives' in the *Guide to the Bedfordshire Record Office* (Bedfordshire County Council, Shire Hall, Bedford. 163 + X pp. 1957) and *Privately-Deposited Records* in the Summary Catalogue of those in the Oxfordshire County Record Office (Oxfordshire County Council, County Hall, Oxford. 158 + X pp. 1966. Record Publication No. 4) are a great quarry or mine of mixed minerals. It would be impossible in one book, never mind in this introduction, to cover all the categories of records which might come up. It may, however, be useful to look at publications which either attempt to give a comprehensive list of documents available for the study of a particular locality or reproduce a representative selection. Examples of the first range from the librarian's *Summary Catalogue of Manuscripts in the Bodleian Library relating to the City, County, and University of Oxford — accessions from 1916 to 1962* (OUP 207 + XIII pp. 1964) to the W E A student's duplicated *Index of Records relating to Farnham* (Council Offices, South Street, Farnham, Surrey. 49 pp. 1965). W O Hassall's *Wheatley Records 956-1956* (Oxfordshire Record Society, 199 pp. 1956) is an admirable selection of records bearing on the history of one parish. There are, of course, many county and regional bibliographies which are, incidentally, guides to local record sources. L R Conisbee's *A Bedfordshire Bibliography* (Bedfordshire Historical Record Society. 332 pp. 1962), *Supplement* (84 pp. 1967) and *Second Supplement* (128 pp. 1971) is an excellent work. Robert Douch's *A Handbook of Local History — Dorset* (University of Bristol Department of Adult Education. 178 pp. 1952. reprint with supplement 1962) is most comprehensive and includes many references to national publications and sources. *A Guide to Regional Studies on the East Riding of Yorkshire and the City of Hull* by A G Dickens and K A Macmahon (Departments of Adult Education and History, The University of Hull, 66 pp. 1956) provides a similar treatment of a quite different part of the country. Alan Jamieson and Brian S Smith have produced in short compass a general introduction to many things the local historian who is a beginner wants to know, in their *Gloucestershire, A Local History Handbook* (Gloucestershire Community Council, 48 pp. 1968).

The central focus around which most privately-deposited records have accumulated is the family estate. There is no simple guide to estate records, but there are guides to the interpretation of title deeds, which are a headache for the student of property: *How to Read Old Title Deeds* by J Cornwall (Department of Extramural Studies, Birmingham. 48 pp. 1964), and *Title Deeds* by A A Dibben (Historical Association, reprinted 1971). R B Pugh's *Calendar of Antrobus Deeds before 1625* (Wiltshire Archaeological Society, 165 + LV pp. 1947) reveals what can be found in one family's papers, as do for a wider date range the catalogues of private archives issued by the West Sussex Record Office at Chichester (cf. *The Petworth House Archives* vol. I 207 + XVI pp. 1968). A J Camp's *Wills and their Whereabouts* (Phillimore. 137

+ XIX pp. 1963) describes the location of wills in different counties and the courts in which they were proved and deposited. Inventories had to be produced when proving a will and the best introduction to them is the edition of *Farm and Cottage Inventories of Mid-Essex 1635-1749* by F W Steer, in particular the long and informative Introduction (Essex Record Office, 312 pp. 1950. reprinted Phillimore 1970). A source which is widely available is maps. F G Emmison's *Catalogue of Maps in the Essex Record Office* (E R O.106 + XX pp. 1947), *First Supplement* (53 + VI pp. 1952), *Second Supplement* (52 + IV pp. 1964) and *Third Supplement* (34 + V pp. 1968), is a very detailed and a pioneer work. P Harvey and H Thorpe produced a study of *The Printed Maps of Warwickshire, 1576-1900* in 1959 (Warwickshire County Council,279 + X pp.), and a similar full list of Shropshire maps appeared in 1960, *The Printed Maps of Shropshire* (Shropshire County Council). *A Catalogue of Manuscript Maps in the Hertfordshire Record Office* by Peter Walne (Hertfordshire County Council, 156 pp. 1969) is not only comprehensive but it gives the surveyor's name and indications of the coverage of each map.

An invaluable source of information for the moderm local historian lies in the printed directories. Jane E Norton's *Guide to the National and Provincial Directories of England and Wales excluding London, published before 1856* has an almost self-explanatory title; it includes notes on some of the publishers (Royal Historical Society, 96 Cheyne Walk, London SW10, 241 + VI pp. 1950). Incidentally, in 1958 the Royal Historical Society also published E L C Mullins' *Texts and Calendars — an analytical guide to serial publications* (674 + XI pp.), which is the place to refer to in order to discover what documents are available in print. There are local studies of directories available, like *Lancashire Directories 1684- 1957* compiled by G H Tupling and S Horrocks (Lancashire Bibliography Committee, Central Library, Manchester 2. 78 + X pp. 1968). Perhaps the most important printed source for modern local history, apart from parliamentary papers, is newspapers. *Newspapers first published before 1900 in Lancashire, Cheshire and the Isle of Man* edited by R E G Smith (The Library Association, 48 pp. 1964) is an excellent example of a county bibliography of local newspapers. *Hertfordshire Newspapers 1772-1955* compiled by M F Thwaite (Hertfordshire Local History Council, 42 pp. duplicated. 1956) like the Lancashire list not only shows what editions of what papers survive but also where they are to be found.

This introduction, like the *Short Guides* which follow, owes a great deal to the experience and wisdom of members of the Local History Committee who have so helped the editor.

Lionel M Munby

Rate Books

Ida Darlington

[Entries from the Poor Rate Books of St. Marylebone (now in St. Marylebone Reference Library) showing the house occupied by Henry Fuseli, the artist. Though it was known from 1797 to 1801 as 75 Queen Anne Street East, it had previously been numbered 72 (evidence from the Rate Book of 1796 not given here) and became, by 1814, No 37 Foley Street. It has been ascertained by careful checking that no subsequent changes have occurred in the numbering of this house.]

1801	1804
Queen Anne Street East	*Queen Anne Street East*
71 F. Bradshaw	71 F. Bradshaw
72 L. Fitzherbert	72 L. Fitzherbert
73 M. Elliott	73 F. Hunt
74 Capt. Bailie	74 R. Marsh
75 *H. Fuseli*	75 *Duke of Lorge*
76. J. G. Wilkinson	76 W. Lupton
77 Smart	77 C. Rayley
78 S. Baxter	78 S. Baxter
79 —	79 S. Pegler

1809	1814
Queen Anne Street East	*Foley Street*
33 J. Landseer	33 J. Landseer
34 C. Echardt	34 C. Echardt
35 F. Hunt	35 F. Hunt
36 C. B. Pasquier	36 C. B. Pasquier
37 *Duke of Lorge*	37 *Duke of Lorge*
38 W. Woods	38 J. Guy
39 J. Morgan	39 S. Harrington
40 J. Lawrence	40 P. F. Le Brun
41 S. Pegler	4I J. Winch

Rates and Rating

A rate is a levy for local purposes based on an assessment of the yearly value of property. Rates of various kinds were levied spasmodically in different parts of the country from at least the fourteenth century onward, e.g. Drainage and Bridge rates, Church rates, etc., and occasionally lists of ratepayers have survived from these levies. Compulsory rating throughout the country had its origin in the 1601 Act for the Relief of the Poor (43 El., c. 2) and its modern definition is still largely based on the terms of that Act. Earlier Acts had, however, been gradually introducing an element of compulsion into the Christian duty of almsgiving, and an Act of I552 (5 and 6 Edw. VI, c. 2) ordered the regular weekly collection of alms in each parish and the entry of such payments in a book, while that of I562-3 (5 El., c. 3) ordered that those who refused to contribute voluntarily should be assessed by the Justices of the Peace to pay a regular weekly sum.

Rate Books

The principle of compulsory rating on property having once been introduced, its use was extended to a variety of purposes, e.g. repair of the highways (Commonwealth Ordinance of 1654, and Acts of 1662, 1670 and 1691), repair of gaols (Act of 11 and 12 Wm. III, c. 19, 1700), etc. Although rates were in practice normally assessed on the value of land and buildings, the doubt as to whether movable property should be rated was not finally resolved until 1840 (Acts 3 and 4 Vic., c. 89). This Act was for one year only but was subsequently renewed from year to year. The long process of change from rating 'according to the ability' of inhabitants to pay to rating according to the annual value of lands and buildings occupied is set out in detail in *The History of Local Rates in England* by E Cannan. The theory that Sewer rates were payable only by owners of lands and tenements which benefited from the sewers remained current until quite recently, but in practice Sewer rates were from an early date levied on occupiers on the assumption, not always justified, that tenants would be able to reclaim the amount from their landlords. Compulsory Church rates were finally abolished in 1868.

Location of Rate Books and their Format

The parish was the normal unit for the collection of Poor and other rates, and rate books are usually to be found with other parish records either in the Church Chest or in the County or Borough Record Office. A few corporate towns early acquired the right of levying rates either for special purposes or for the relief of the poor and the rate books should, therefore, be with the borough records. Rate books, perhaps because of their number and bulk, have mostly had a low survival value in the eyes of their custodians and it is rare to find anything like a complete series covering the seventeenth and eighteenth centuries. Survivals of the voluntary Poor rate books of the sixteenth century are even rarer but examples are to be found from the Cities of London and Westminster and from Southwark, and occasionally from the central parishes of other old towns. These are separate books and are not to be confused with lists of contributors to the poor which occur in Churchwardens' Accounts and which are usually arranged by precedence and not according to the location of the contributors' dwellings. In 1744 an Act (17 Geo. II, c. 3) gave residents the right to inspect rate books, and series sometimes begin from this date.

Church rate books, Scavengers' rate books, etc., may be found to fill in gaps in the Poor rate books. In the London area the Sewer rate books in the London County Record Office are useful for this purpose though a Sewer rate was not levied every year and few books exist for the period prior to 1700. The Sewer rate books sometimes include the names of owners as well as of occupiers of property.

Early rate books were often bound in parts of old parchment deeds. Later, school exercise books were sometimes used. Books printed specially for the purpose with columns and headings gradually came into use during the later part of the eighteenth century. Sometimes the occupation or profession of the ratepayer is entered or a brief description is given of the property, e.g. 'House, barn and garden'. Occasionally rate collectors made notes on the margins or interleaving of their books — such as 'gone', 'run away', 'poor' or more helpfully for modern searchers, such remarks as 'house puld down and rebuilt' and 'in the markett a bacon shop at the corner'. These examples are from the

Sewer rate books of Westminster Commission of Sewers 1711 and 1718 in the London County Record Office.

The Uses of Rate Books

Rate books contain lists of householders and/or owners, with an assessment of the value of their properties and the amount to be collected from them. Their primary use for the local historian is to give the names of families and individuals living in a parish and the number of occupied houses or tenements. From them it is often possible to find out when houses were first occupied and by inference the approximate date of their erection, and also the date when particular street names came into use. Normally, for the convenience of the collectors, the houses were listed road by road or street by street so that even before the roads were named or any numbering system was introduced the location of individual properties can be traced if the series of books is sufficiently complete, but much time and patience may be required. For this purpose the rate books are a much more complete record than are street directories since these, even for important towns, are seldom arranged by streets before 1840. Earlier directories are usually only lists of traders, and later of private residents, arranged alphabetically. These early directories, which for large towns often begin during the last quarter of the eighteenth century, may, however, be a useful check on deductions arrived at through the rate books. Even after 1840 street directories are of limited value in suburban areas and small towns for which they were only published intermittently.

If it is desired to trace the occupants and dates of a particular house, referred to here as X, the best plan is to work backwards. For the twentieth century, street directories may be a short cut but it is never safe to assume without working back steadily that there has been no change of numbering. In the Metropolitan Area a register of all naming and numbering changes has been kept since 1856, and is now maintained by the Architect to the London County Council. The dates, though not the exact details of such changes, are listed in the *London County Council Names of streets and places in the administrative county of London*, 1955. Even in the County of London a few suburban streets remained unnumbered until late in the last century. The most methodical way of tracing back through the rate books, and the quickest in the long run, is to divide sheets of lined paper into columns, to list at least three names on either side of X so as to be sure of continuity, and to copy out the entries for each year or half year in which there is a change in the occupant of X. Where the same occupier is listed over a long period intermediate extracts should be taken as an additional check.

If, on the other hand, it is desired to trace which existing house was formerly the residence of a particular person Y (or stands on the site of his residence) then the earliest entry containing his name should be copied, again with at least three names on either side, and the houses should be traced forward. Normally it is sufficient to take out entries for every fifth year provided that the continuity is ensured. The example given on page 12 shows some of the pitfalls which may arise. During the period 1801-14 there was both a change of numbering and, in a different year, a change of street name, but in each case sufficient names have been extracted to ensure that the required house, i.e. the residence of Henry Fuseli, has been correctly identified.

The numbering of houses in London was authorised by a series of Acts for paving, cleansing and improving the streets. The first, passed in 1767 (8 Geo. III, c. 21), applied only to the City and its liberties, but it was quickly followed by others relating to St. Marylebone, St. Pancras, etc. The numbers were frequently changed up to at least as late as 1830, and any comparisons with the numbering given in, e.g. Boyle's *Court Guides* or on Horwood's maps of London, must be made with caution. Outside London, numbering did not come into use until later. The first general Act authorising its adoption was the Towns Improvement Act of 1847 (10 and 11 Vic., c. 34).

When the rate books do not include house numbers the amount of the assessments should be extracted instead, since any violent fluctuation in the assessment of an individual house provides a warning either that it may have been wrongly identified or that rebuilding or major alterations have been carried out. Other sources of difficulty in identifying houses are (i) the numbering or listing of corner houses sometimes in one street and sometimes in another, (2) the combination of two houses into one or the splitting of one house into two or more, (3) the awkward trait of some collectors (or rate book compilers) of occasionally altering their route so that the names in certain streets may be listed in reverse order, (4) the practice adopted in London, as suburban parishes grew, of splitting them into 'divisions', which were sometimes re-defined, so that in succeeding years a street disappears from one portion of a rate book and reappears in another. Unfortunately some rate books lack comprehensive or even divisional street indexes, and a thorough search may be necessary to find the new location of a particular street.

Bibliography

Cannan, E, *The History of Local Rates in England*, 1927

Tate, W E, *The Parish Chest*, 1960

There are few printed lists of rate books but those for the City of London are included in **London Rate Assessments and Inhabitants Lists in Guildhall Library and the Corporation of London Records Office**, issued by the Corporation in 1960, and those for Westminster in J E Smith's **A Catalogue of Westminster Records**, 1900, and W Mason's **Catalogue of Books and Documents Belonging to the Royal Parish of St. Martin-in-the-Fields**.

Poll Books

John Cannon

[From the poll book for the election at Norwich, 15 May 1734, the candidates being Sir Edward Ward, Bt., Miles Brandthwayt, Horace Walpole and Waller Bacon.]

ST. PAUL'S PARISH	Ward	Brant.	Walp.	Bacon
Barnes John, *Worsted-weaver*			—	—
Bell Thomas, *Gent.*		—		
Benham John, *Worsted-weaver*		—	—	
Blyth Richard, *Worsted-weaver*		—	—	
Blyth William, *Gent.*		—	—	
Briggs Robert, *Carpenter*		—	—	
Butcher Ezekiel, *Wool-comber*			—	—
Carr Richard, *Baker*		—	—	
Castell Peter, *Barber*		—		
Cheanna Richard, *Freeholder St. Paul's*	—	—		
Clarke Edward, *Freeholder St. Paul's*			—	—
Cockadey Peter, *Worsted-weaver*			—	—
Cockman John, *Barber*		—	—	
Coe John, *Worsted-weaver*			—	—

Poll Books

Immediately after the General Election of 1695, a bill was introduced to prevent irregular proceedings by returning officers. One of the provisions of the bill, which received the royal assent on 10 April 1696, was that returning officers should deliver on request a copy of the poll 'at a reasonable charge for writing the same'. The intention was to guarantee, at a time when returning officers were notoriously partial, that electors should have access to the records in order to establish their claims: the printer of the Norwich poll book quoted above expressed the hope that it would 'be of great service both in taking and scrutinizing future polls'. Poll books continued to be published until the introduction of secret voting in 1872, the first election to be conducted by the ballot being at Pontefract on 17 August. The last general election for which poll books are available was that of 1868, and it was partly because of illegal practices during this election that the campaign for the ballot succeeded.

Poll Books and their Format

Before long returning officers seem to have left it to local printers to satisfy any demand for copies, and most poll books were published as commercial ventures, largely to gratify curiosity. That for the Hertfordshire election of 1727, however, was published by the two successful candidates, and the Kent poll book for 1734 was published by subscription. It cannot be assumed that a poll book was published for every contested election: indeed, there would be little need for a poll book at Malmesbury, where until the Reform Act of 1832 the electors numbered 13, or at Orford where there were 12. The printer of the poll book for Cambridge University (1780) claimed that he was performing a public service by placing the votes on record 'in order that everyone might judge of the principles and form conjectures of the motives of each elector ... It has been suggested to the writer of this advertisement that the publication of this poll might offend some persons in the University. To which he answers, that he neither fears the resentment nor values the friendship of any elector who is ashamed that the world should know in what manner he voted.'

The information given varies from book to book, each printer deciding what was worth including. The poll book for Oxford City (1802) gives names, addresses, occupations and votes, together with a list of freemen who did not record a vote. The poll book for Newcastle-on-Tyne (1741), on the other hand, gives no addresses, but divides up the voters according to their occupations — bakers, weavers, plumbers and the like. In poll books for county elections it was customary to print the lists in the alphabetical order of parishes, or by Hundreds, giving the names, residences, place and nature of freehold, and the occupier. Some books, particularly in the later period, include an account of the campaign: the poll book for Liverpool (1780) prints 103 pages of speeches, letters, ballads, advertisements and election abuse. But most books confine themselves to the voting record. Quite often copies were used by election agents for canvassing purposes, and it is not uncommon to find marginal notes and comments.

Location

Several thousands of poll books are still in existence. The Institute of Historical Research has more than 500; the Bodleian, the Guildhall Library and the British Museum have large collections, and more are to be found in county record offices, reference libraries, local museums and among private papers. In most large boroughs there was sufficient demand for good runs to be extant today. Between the years 1741 and 1872, for example, there are poll books surviving for 29 elections at Colchester, 28 at Norwich and Maidstone, 26 at Ipswich, 25 at Hull, 24 at Coventry, 22 at Shrewsbury and Lincoln, and 21 at Rochester and Cambridge. In boroughs where the electorate was small, such as Salisbury, voting lists were often printed in the local newspapers. Even where no published poll books are in existence, the original manuscripts are sometimes preserved, particularly in county record offices.

The Uses of Poll Books

A single copy of a poll book is not necessarily of great assistance to the historian. It will give the election result, but this can often be more conveniently found in H Stooks Smith, *The Parliaments of England*, or in contemporary newspapers. It may, however, be of importance to ascertain whether certain candidates were running in harness, and this will easily be seen from the voting pattern. Similarly, the geographical distribution of the votes may be significant, particularly in county elections. An analysis of the Warwickshire contest of 1774 between John Mordaunt, Thomas Skipwith and Sir Charles Holte, demonstrates that Holte drew his support overwhelmingly from Birmingham and district, and confirms that the dissenting and commercial interest was making a deliberate attempt to wrest one of the county seats from the landed gentry. To take an example from a borough, an examination of the Honiton poll book (1763) shows how wide the franchise could be in the potwalloper boroughs. There is not one esquire recorded: the electorate, which must have included most adult males, was made up of labourers, artisans and small shopkeepers. Even historians who are not interested in parliamentary affairs may find poll books helpful. Where occupations are given, they can yield evidence about local industries, while the number of freeholders voting for any given place affords some indication of the population. For example, the poll book for Wiltshire (1705) shows 46 freeholders voting from Purton and 26 from the neighbouring village of Swindon: in 1819 Purton produced 91 votes and Swindon 59. Today, after the coming of the railway industry to Swindon, the respective populations are 2400 and 80,000.

The value of poll books is, however, greatly increased if they can be analysed as part of a series, or in conjunction with other sources. An examination of the Hertfordshire poll book of 1761 helps to explain how Thomas Plumer Byde was able to defeat a coalition of the Whigs and Tories, supported by the leading men of property in the county. He appealed to the irreconcilables on either side to spurn the compromise, and came top of the poll with the aid of the Dissenters and the lesser Tories. The distribution of the Tory vote can be traced by comparing the poll book with that of 1754, when a single Tory candidate was standing.

Perhaps the best way to illustrate the use of poll books in conjunction with other material is to refer to two recent articles. Dr Rudé, in his article 'The Middlesex Electors Of 1768-1769' (*Eng. Hist. Review*, Oct. 1960) has correlated the Middlesex poll book with the Land Tax assessments, the Freeholders' Book and the Poor Rate books, in order to throw light on Wilkes' supporters. He demonstrates that by 1768 the urban London area outweighed the rural parts of the county, and that Wilkes owed his victory to the support he received from the urban voters, particularly those of East London. The voting pattern emphasises the determined hostility towards Wilkes of the propertied and professional classes.

One disadvantage of this particular poll book is that it does not give occupations, but this can to some extent be overcome by correlating it with the various trade directories of the period. It can then be demonstrated that Wilkes drew a good deal of his support from the smaller tradesmen and shopkeepers. A revealing comparison can be made between the larger merchants (brokers, directors, brewers, bankers), who inclined strongly to the court, and the smaller (grocers, chemists, cheesemongers, upholsterers, undertakers), who voted for Wilkes. This helps to explain how Wilkes was able to achieve his totally unexpected victory in the face of the most powerful influence. An analysis on a different level reveals that scores of members of parliament and placemen, devoted adherents of the court, did not trouble to vote at the first election, and suggests that the court candidates seriously underestimated the challenge of Wilkes at first.

My own article, 'The Wiltshire Election of 1772: an Interpretation' (*Wiltshire Archaeological Magazine*, lviii), deals with the celebrated contest between Ambrose Goddard and Henry Herbert, which has always been regarded as a spontaneous revolt of the ordinary freeholders against aristocratic domination. Here it was possible to compare the voting, as given by the poll book, with the forecasts made by the gentlemen who formed Goddard's campaign committee. The forecasts coincided with the actual results to such a nicety as to make it clear that very few freeholders could have had any independence of their landlords. Moreover, a detailed analysis of the voting brought out the political character of the contest, which had previously been disregarded. Twenty members of parliament voted, and it can be seen that Goddard was supported as the avowed champion of the opposition to Lord North's administration. A further comparison with the supporters of the campaign for economical reform (whose names could be traced from local newspapers) confirmed this.

Bibliography

For election results: ***The Official Return of MPs 1213-1874*** (1879)

Judd IV, G P, *Members of Parliament 1734-1852* (1955)

McCalmont, F H, *The Parliamentary Poll Book of all Elections 1832-1906* (1906)

For a modern edition of a poll book: ***Poll Books of Nottingham and Nottinghamshire, 1710*** (Thoroton Soc. Rec. Ser. xviii, 1958)

The following works throw light on electoral mechanics, or make extensive use of poll books:

Bonsall, B, *Sir James Lowther and Cumberland and Westmorland Elections* (1960)

Forrester, E G, *Northamptonshire County Elections and Electioneering 1695-1832* (1941)

Gash, N, *Politics in the Age of Peel* (1953)

Hanham, H J, *Elections and Party Management* (1959)

Namier, L B, *The Structure of Politics at the Accession of George III* (2nd edit. 1957)

Neale, J E, *The Elizabethan House of Commons* (1949)

Oldfield, T B H, *History of the Boroughs* (1792)

Porritt, E, *The Unreformed House of Commons* (1903)

Robson, R J, *The Oxfordshire Election of 1754* (1949)

Rudé, G, *Wilkes and Liberty* (1962)

Probate Inventories

Francis W Steer

[Inventory and valuation of the effects of John Brooms, village blacksmith, of North Mundham, now in the Diocesan Record Office, Chichester. Brooms was buried on 18 March 1732/3; on the 30th John Strudwick and William Stowell made the inventory; almost a year later, on 2 March 1733/4, this was exhibited to Thomas Ball, prebendary of Eartham in Chichester Cathedral, Surrogate, who granted letters of administration to the deceased's brother, William Brooms. The transcript closely follows the original document in regard to spelling, use of capital letters and abbreviations; some punctuation has been introduced and noughts omitted from sums of money.]

A True & perfect Inventory of all & singular the goods Chattles & Creditts of John Brooms late of the parish of Northmundham in the County of Sussex Blacksmith dec'ed Taken valued & appraised By John Strudwick & William Stowell the 30th day of March In the year of our Lord 1733.
IMPRIMIS In the Lower Chamber. One Bed, a press & Chest of Drawes, 8*li*.; Seven Chaires, A Glass & Earthenware, 11*s*.; Curtaines, Rodds, a looking glass & a Cubbord, 5*s*.
In the Fire Room. A Clock & small things over the mantle, 2*li*. 13*s*.; A jack & things in the Corners & Two tables & a Cubbord, 3*li*.; 7 Chaires, 1 Chest & joint Stool, Glasses & Books, 16*s*.; The Shelves, bacon rack, 3 flitches & One peice of bacon, 4*li*. 6*s*.; Sixty pound of butter, 1*li*. 15*s*.
In the Hall. Two desks, Table & Chaires, 3*s*.
In the Sellar. Vessells & beer, 1*li*. 10*s*.
In the Pantry. Two powdering Tubbs, Pork, Salting Trough, Stand, 2 Shelves & 3 Cheeses, 1*li*. 10*s*.
In the brewhouse. A Furnace & brewing Vessells, 4*li*. 10*s*. In the Chambers. One bed, a Chest & boxes, 1 *li*. 10*s*.; Another bed & 11 Sheets, 3*li*. 2*s*.; Wearing Apparell, A Chest, 2 boxes & a Table, 1 *li*. 8*s*.
A Horse, Two Hoggs & Two Stalls of bees, 4*li*. 12*s*. Bellows in the Shop & Coldtrow, 2*li*. 10*s*.; $^1/_2$ Hundred Weight of Tongs & Steel, 1*li*. 2*s*. 8*d*.; Two Hundred Weight & 4 lbs of new Iron, 1*li*. 9*s*. 2*d*.; Hammers, Sledges & small Tools, 1*li*. 17*s*. 6*d*.; The Hanvill & Two backirons, 4*li*. 4*s*. 9*d*.; Two Stocks & 8 Blocks & a Spring Tool, 17*s*.; Twenty small Tools, 5*s*.; One Hundred & $^1/_2$ of old Iron & Chaines, 1 *li*. 8*s*.; 1500 Hundred of [*blank*] Iron, 11*li*. 5*s*.; 200 Weight of old Iron, 18*s*. 8*d*.; 35 lbs. of new Iron, 6*s*. 8*d*.; New Horse Shoes weighing 100 pounds, 1*li*. 9 *s*. 2*d*.; Old Stock Bonds & Shoes, 17*s*.; Boxes & Shoeing Tools, 10*s*.; One Hundred & $^1/_2$ of old Iron, 13*s*. 6*d*.; A grinding Stone & Trough, 10*s*.; Prongstaves, Rakes & Shovell Trees, 1*li*. 1*s*. 6*d*.; Cools, 1*li*. 0*s*. 3*d*.; 3 Half Hundred Weights & $^3/_4$ of a Hundred of Lead Weights, 1*li*. 12*s*.; Beams & Scales, 8*s*.; The Vice, Bench & old Files, 8*s*.; A Shovell & Scraps of Iron, 5*s*. 6*d*.; Lumber in the House & Shopp, 7*s*. 6*d*.
Sum tot' is 74*li*. 17*s*. 10*d*.
2^d March 1733 William Brooms natural & lawfull Brother of the said dec'ed & Administrator &c was sworne &c. Bcfore me, Tho. Ball, Surrogate.

Location

At the time of probate or administration being granted, executors or administrators were required to produce to the court an inventory of the deceased's goods, chattels and credits, not only for the protection of the executors and the relatives of the deceased, but as a basis for the calculation of court fees. The inventories were usually made up into large bundles, sometimes threaded on a thong, and kept by the appropriate registrar with the wills. With the establishment of Diocesan Record Offices, large quantities of inventories have now become available for study instead of being difficult of access in Diocesan Registries. The inventories exhibited in the Prerogative Court of Canterbury, mostly of the eighteenth century, are in the custody of the Principal Probate Registry, at Somerset House. It is understood that a list is in preparation with a view to making the documents accessible to the public. B. G. Bouwens, in his *Wills and their whereabouts* (I939), noted the existence of inventories in Registries, and it is hoped that the revised edition of this useful handbook will give similar and up-to-date information.

The Uses of Inventories

What sort of picture are we able to draw from inventories? Taking John Brooms as an example, we find that his house was a modest establishment comprising a principal bedroom, a living room with a fireplace, a hall (too grand a name for what was probably only a passageway or a very small room), a cellar, pantry, brewhouse and perhaps two more tiny bedrooms. The furnishings of these rooms were sparse but relatively highly priced at £34.19s.0d., of which £6. 1s 0. was represented by bacon and butter; an unknown figure is included for deceased's wearing apparel. It will be noticed that curtains, a looking glass, a clock and some books are among the items listed; such homely objects would not have been found in the house of a man of similar social standing fifty or sixty years earlier. The large stock of bacon and butter is noteworthy and the brewing utensils suggest that Brooms filled the dual capacities of blacksmith and brewer in his parish.

Turning to the trade and outdoor effects we find that these were valued at £39.18s.10d.If we exclude the value of the livestock we are left with trade tools and stock worth £35.6s.10d. The contents of the blacksmith's shop are interesting because we get the names of objects, their value and quantities. For example, new iron was worth between about 14s. and £1 a hundredweight while old iron was less than 10s. a hundredweight. Approximately a hundredweight of iron turned into horseshoes brought the blacksmith 10s. for his labour and fuel. The bellows and the trough for cooling the smith's work were worth just over half the value of the anvil and the 'backirons'. (This word 'backirons' is often written as 'beckhorn', a corruption of 'bicorne', an anvil with two horns, or cones, at its ends for shaping iron to a curve; see p. 347 of L F Salzman, *Building in England down to 1540* (Oxford, 1952).) The smith kept a stock of handles for pitchforks, rakes and shovels.

The spelling of many inventories is often phonetic, but the interpretation of local forms of words comes with practice and the use of dialect dictionaries. Trade terms present greater problems but the *OED* and various specialist dictionaries often give the answers. Whatever the period of the inventory or the status of the person to whose goods it relates, there is no doubt that, if used with discretion, it can provide information not easily gathered elsewhere. More important, however, is the value of a long series of inventories relating to one parish or one trade; Mr. G. H. Kenyon's handling and assessment of the material for the large rural parish of Kirdford and the small country town of Petworth is a model for all future workers with this class of archive.

The idea has developed that probate inventories are an infallible guide to the sizes of houses, their entire contents, the wealth of their occupiers and the productivity of the land. This is not so, because we have no guarantee that the appraisers listed every room in a house (and why should they record the existence of an empty room or one that contained nothing of value?), that they listed every item in the house or its precincts, or that they were uniformly careful to give an impartial and precise valuation. We have no certain way of judging the competence of appraisers or of knowing how seriously they fulfilled their duties. A probate inventory must therefore be regarded as a useful, but approximate guide; due attention must be given to the time of year when an inventory was made of the goods of a yeoman or other person concerned with crops and livestock. When using inventories for the agrarian history of a county, special care must be exercised to recognise farming regions, or the comparative results obtained for various parts of a county will be hopelessly inaccurate and misleading. With the growth of interest in agrarian history, it may be worth pointing out to potential users of inventories that a knowledge of what the region under review is capable of producing should be obtained from a practical farmer; it is too easy to write an impressive historical study on farming which proves entirely unrealistic when closely examined by an expert who knows the land. Random sampling is dangerous: what is wanted are more and more detailed investigations on lines similar to that for Kirdford mentioned above.

Probate inventories give us an immense range of information. Where else could we get such evidence for the development of, and changes in, household furnishings, the improvement of living conditions, the incidence of particular trades, the names and values of a multitude of objects and goods which reflect the day-today needs of all types of society? Used in conjunction with wills, title-deeds and other archives, probate inventories abound in that essential human background so difficult to achieve.

Another aspect worth mentioning is that demanded by the specialist. There is an incredible amount of information to be gained from inventories concerning physicians, surgeons and apothecaries, from those of men following purely local trades such as the needlemakers of Chichester or the stone-workers of Purbeck, from those who were merchants in Norwich or Ipswich, from those who were gardeners, men of letters, jewellers, maltsters or engaged in producing or selling the requirements of ordinary men and women. Then there is the fascination of knowing about the contents of rich men's houses, where may appear wearing apparel, pictures, plate, furnishings and other treasures such as are now exhibited with justifiable pride in our national museums.

Bibliography

The duty of executors and administrators in making an inventory is given by Richard Burn in his *Ecclesiastical Law* (1760 and later editions) under the subject of wills.

Ashmore, O and **Bagley, J J**, 'Inventories as a Source of Local History', *The Amateur Historian*, iv (1959-60) pp 157-61, 186-95, 227-31

Barley, M W, *The English Farmhouse and Cottage* (Routledge and Kegan Paul, London, 1961)

Emmison, F G, *Jacobean Household Inventories* (Beds. Historical Record Society, xx, 1938)

Hoskins, W G, *The Midland Peasant* (Macmillan, London, 1957)

Kenyon, G H, 'Kirdford Inventories, 1611 to 1776', in *Sussex Archaeological Collections*, xciii (1955), pp 78-156

Kenyon, G H, 'Petworth Town and Trades, 1610-1760, in *Sussex Archaeological Collections*, xcvi (1958), pp35-107. xcviii (1959), pp 71-117, xcix (1961), pp 102-48

Steer, F W, *Farm and Cottage Inventories of Mid-Essex, 1635-1749* (Essex Record Office, Chelmsford, 1950)

Steer, F W, 'The Inventory of Arthur Coke of Bramfield, 1629', in *Proceedings of the Suffolk Institute of Archaeology*, xxv, part iii (1951), pp 264-87

Steer, F W, 'The Inventory of Anne, Viscountess Dorchester, 1638-9,' in *Notes & Queries* (OUP), vols. cxcviii, cxcix (in instalments)

Steer, F W, 'Smaller Houses and their Furnishings in the Seventeenth and Eighteenth Centuries', in the *Journal of the British Archaeological Association*, Third Series, xx, xxi (1957-8), pp 140-59

Steer, F W, 'The Possessions of a Sussex Surgeon', in *Medical History*, ii (1958), pp 134-6

Estate Maps and Surveys

F G Emmison

[From a survey of the Manor of Felsted, Essex, 1577: Essex Record Office,D/DCw M158/3.]

THE MANNOUR OF FELSTED

A Survey of the Mannour of Felsted and of all and singular the lands tennements messuages demeasnes yards barnes pigeon houses orchards gardens ponds fisheryes mills arrable lands meadows marsh and pasture woods underwoods wasts and wast ground rents and other hereditaments whatsoever belonging to the aforesaid mannour or in any other kind belonging or appertaineing thereunto as well the free and customary tennants as the demesne lands of the said mannour, made by Edward Worstley gent. in the 19th yeare of the raigne of Queen Elizabeth, as well by the view of the lands tennements and other hereditaments aforesaid and perambulation of the said mannour as by the oathes of William Browne [and 15 other named] tennants of the said mannour to this corporally sworne. A briefe or abstract of the libertyes of the Mannour of Felsted parcell of the possession late of the Abby of Syon. The Lord Rich claimes for himselfe and his tennants in his right to enjoy Court Leet etc., the Assise of Bread Wine and Beer, Weighing of Weights etc., Pillary, Tumbrell, Stocks, Wafts and Strayes, Treasure Trove, Deodands, by prescription.

[Freehold tenants]

Thomas Wiseman gent. holds free by charter in free socage, as it is said but is not yet shewn, one close of arrable land called Orpich alias Orpins land containeing by estimation 8 acres, lying between the coppyhold lands of William Olmsted called Berland on the east part and ... Acreman Lane on the west part, one head thereof abutting upon the coppyhold land of the said Thomas Wiseman called Martens land on the south part, and another head thereof abutting upon the land of the said William Olmsted called Wedyes on the north part....

Humphry Bridge holds free in free socage by charter the 5th of August in 1st yeare of Queen Elizabeth one tennement called Barbors one barne one stable one small curtilage and two small orchards containeing together $\frac{1}{2}$ acre lying next to the land of the lord of the mannour called Blackley and a certaine croft of arrable land of the said Humphry's on the south part, and to Vary Green on the north part, to Blackley Gate on the west part, and to the land of Thomas Clarke on the east part; and one croft of arrable land containeing by estimation $3\frac{1}{2}$ acres lying behind the said tennement between the land of the lord of the mannour aforesaid called Blackley aforesaid on the east and west parts, one end thereof abutting upon Blackley aforesaid on the south part, and another end thereof abutting upon the aforesaid tennement called Barbors on the north part.

[And 90 similar entries describing the freeholds.]

[Copyhold tenants]

John Bridge holds by coppy of court roll dated the 9th of December in the 3rd yeare of Queen Elizabeth one tennement called Beles one kitchen behind the said tennement covered with tyles one barne and one stable covered with straw and one garden and one curtilage containeing in the whole $\frac{1}{2}$ acre, lying together between the land parcell of the halfe yard land called Hurtlings halfe yard on the west and south part, to Beles green on the east part, and a lane called Coleshall lane on the north part.

Estate Maps and Surveys

[And 17 similar entries describing the copyholds, followed by brief sections dealing with rents from the leased demesne and tithes, with the liberties, customs and boundaries of the manor, with the lord's rights to fishing and fowling and the holding of courts, and a detailed description of the common and rights of common within the manor.]

Surveys and Maps: Origin and Location

Large numbers of estate maps and surveys have been 'discovered' and acquired by local record offices in the past thirty years; they are still being received at an encouraging rate. Descriptive *surveys* antedate local estate *maps*, which, apart from a few somewhat crude examples, do not appear as accurate records much before 1550 and are scarce until about 1600. Really full local surveys, like maps, are rare before 1550, but surveys with less detail for the two preceding centuries are not uncommon. Written descriptions of many manors and larger estates are available in the national and local archive repositories, and are termed extents, rentals, terriers and surveys. Only if they give names of holdings or fields and abuttals (bounds of holdings or fields), as well as tenants' names, is their topographical value high. Detailed and accurate surveys and maps both originate shortly before 1600 with the gradual emergence of a new profession of surveyors, who knew some manorial law and Latin as well as practical mathematics including use of theodolite and plane-table.

A survey *may* be amplified by a map; if so, the latter is either a separate document, or is sewn into the survey roll or book, or is in the form of several or many small maps of farms or even single closes drawn opposite or near to the relevant entries in the survey. A map *may* be amplified by a written description, varying from the reference table (to numbers on the map) giving merely field-names and acreages to elaborate detail such as the state of cultivation of every field and kinds of trees in hedgerows. But, although related in their contents, surveys and maps do not usually accompany each other and in some respects may differ in their *raison d'être*.

Surveys and their Format

The great majority are manorial surveys, which were compiled by the steward or by a surveyor, from oral testimony of the older tenants or jurors, often supplemented by written evidence of earlier extents, rentals, court rolls and deeds. Some surveys include brief extracts from much older documents and may even trace tenants backwards to the fourteenth century with significant facts for earlier topographical history. A manorial survey may concern itself primarily with the lord's demesne, with perhaps a brief description of manor-house, park, windmill, dovecote, parsonage, woods, commons, greens, heaths or wastes, fisheries, boundary, and customs of the manor. Or it may comprise an account of the copyholds and freeholds, without any description of the demesne. It may also reveal interesting facts about market and fairs, school and free chapel, church and advowson, glebe and tithes, newly 'inned' marshes, timber, enclosure of commons or open fields, depopulation, disparking, and so on. The kind of information which one hopes to find in a fairly detailed survey is of course partly related to geographical and other physical factors. It will emphasise the inherent topographical (as well as economic) differences between manors with open-field or enclosed, urban or rural, nucleated or discrete, low-lying or moorland, forest, pastoral, coastal or other characteristics. One will find vital differences between the survey of a Kent manor and that of a manor in (say) East Anglia, the West Country or the Midlands. The survey of a highly organised manor with a large population, though not necessarily a borough or even having a market, will probably yield much information which is lacking in that of a small, remote manor.

The entries in an urban manor survey may be arranged street by street and constitute an early 'directory'. Surveys range in length from a single sheet of parchment or paper to a long parchment or paper roll or rolled file, or a massive volume. Those of the seventeenth century or earlier may be in Latin; some as early as 1450 are in English.

Maps

The 'New Men' who arose after the suppression of the religious houses needed expert surveyors to describe and map their estates. Christopher Saxton, John Norden, Ralph Agas and John Walker are among the Elizabethan surveyor-cartographers who achieved a degree of cartographical accuracy as well as artistic merit which stands the sternest tests: for instance, the many Essex manor and estate maps of John Walker senior and junior around 1590-1615 have survived the most thorough examination and can be used with confidence in the smallest details, even the position of the cottage windows.

By the eighteenth century much attention was given to elaborately worded or eulogistical titles and heraldic achievements in full colour. Nearly all estate maps show buildings in block plan, names, acreages and boundaries of fields, roads and lanes, and rivers and streams. A fair proportion of maps indicate the state of cultivation of each field by colour, by shading, or in words; distinction between deciduous and coniferous woods and between meadow and pasture is much rarer. In some, parks and ornamental gardens are carefully drawn. Vineyards, hopgrounds, saffron-grounds, melon-grounds, and so forth may be marked. The many distinctive characteristics of open or common fields and meadows are usually shown. If the estate is small, only the strips and doles of the owner may be drawn; but the big landowner of an open-field parish or manor usually commissioned a complete strip-map. Buildings shown in block plan may be drawn to exact scale. Before the eighteenth century, but less commonly thereafter, they may be represented in miniature perspective view instead of in block plan. (The Walkers' Essex maps combine both plan and elevation with astonishingly beautiful effect.) Bird's-eye views or sketches are usually confined to the more important buildings — manor-house, church, farmhouses, windmills; and some of these little pictures are the only visual representation of vanished churches and mills. The student will try to assess from other features their probable degree of accuracy.

The Uses of Surveys and Maps

The uses to which estate surveys and maps can be put are manifold. Particular buildings or sites can be traced and dated. Field patterns can be studied — the progressive enclosure of open fields, the fragmentation over the years of large enclosed fields or, conversely, the opening out of small crofts and closes into large fields, together with the relationship of these changes to land use, agricultural practice and landowners' policy. Settlement distribution can be examined in relation to population analysis. Apparent anomalies in field boundaries or road systems may be explained by eighteenth-century estate maps showing landscape planning of parks which led to highways diversions (these can be checked in the records of the Clerk of the Peace). In counties with a marshy seaboard the maps of marshland farms can throw light on the stages of reclamation. Finally, detailed surveys giving abuttals and acreages can be used to make maps at periods for which no maps exist. This last is long, patient work, involving the accurate identification of each holding described in the survey (helped by manor court records, estate maps at other dates and deeds) with its counterpart on ordnance survey maps and tithe maps.

Bibliography

Handlist of Record Publications (Brit. Rec. Ass., Publications Pamphlet 3, 1951) gives a selection of surveys in print.

Detailed catalogues of maps in the Bedfordshire and Essex Record Offices (Beds. and Essex County Councils, between 1930 and 1952) include also enclosure and tithe award maps, canal and railway maps, and (Essex only) manorial surveys.

Lynam, E. *The Mapmaker's Art* (1953) has a short section on estate maps, and **Emmison, F G,** *The Art of the Mapmaker in Essex* (1947), relates mainly to estate maps and manorial surveys.

Guardians' Minute Books

Jane M Coleman

[Extract from the minutes of the Board of Guardians of Westbourne Union, Sussex (West Sussex Record Office, WG11/1/1)]

At a weekly meeting of the Board of Guardians of the Westbourne Union held at the workhouse at Westbourne on Friday the 5th June 1835. Present: Edward Bold Esquire the Chairman; John Cousens (Westbourne), Edward Wyatt (North and Up Marden), James Smith (Stoughton), Thomas Hipkin (Racton), George Porcher (Funtington), Edward and Thomas Bennett (Bosham), David Padwick (West Thorney) .... John Green of Stoughton ordered to work on the roads .... Elizabeth Elliott of Compton of imbecile mind residing at Wisborough Green ordered to be relieved with 5s today and 3s. a week in future without coming into the Union. Richard Greentree of Compton ordered to lose a fortnight's relief for incivility to the relieving officer .... Lucy wife of Thomas Pearce belonging to Westbourne ordered to be relieved as a widow while her husband is in prison .... Wm. Bulbeck of Racton ordered to go into the Westbourne Workhouse. George Stevens of Westbourne ordered to be relieved with 1/6 weekly on account of his wife's illness ....

Ordered that the Clerk do write to the Assistant Commissioner requesting him to enquire why the Mills [*for grinding bones. A common way of occupying the poor in the workhouse*] he had ordered have not been furnished .... Ordered that an advertisement for a Governor and Matron of the Workhouse .... [for] the reception of aged persons be inserted in both the Portsmouth newspapers and that it state that they must be man and wife without incumbrance and that their 'joint salary will £25 and that testimonials and applications must be sent to the workhouse by 10 o'clock on Friday next. Ordered that the Governor of the Westbourne workhouse do purchase two dozen of large pans and two dozen of small for the use of the workhouse ....

The Background to the Poor Law Amendment Act, 1834

Until the passing of the 1834 Act, which brought about the formation of the Boards of Guardians, poor relief had, except in a few places where 'Gilbert Unions' had been set up under an earlier permissive Act of 1782, been the responsibility of parish overseers, answerable to the justices in Quarter Sessions, but in practice largely independent. The paupers were therefore at the mercy of amateur and often illiterate officers, and although some overseers acted with humanity and generosity within their limitations, the system was, by the end of the eighteenth century, in hopeless confusion. Under the influence of the war and bad harvests, as well as the inherent defects of the system, poor rates mounted and the benefit to the poor from the sums of money collected grew less; employers paid starvation wages, as they knew that labourers could always get monetary assistance from the parish if necessary. It was, in fact, often more profitable for the lazy labourer to be completely out of work and dependent on the overseers. In towns, slum landlords prospered, for the rents of pauper tenants were paid by the parish authorities, and the landlords were not required to pay poor-rates on such property.

After a number of abortive attempts at reform, such as the Sturges Bourne Acts, a Royal Commission was set up to investigate poor relief in 1832, and as a result of its deliberations the Poor Law Amendment Act was passed. Despite general agreement that the country was facing ruin as a result of the increase of pauperism, and incompetence and corruption in the administration of the existing poor law, it must not be imagined that the provisions of the Act were arrived at easily. There was available to the Commission of Enquiry a whole range, stretching back over several decades, of stated opinion and report from such people as Henry Fielding, Eden, Bentham, Malthus, Ricardo, Sturges Bourne, and many less well known. Some looked for the cure in new or amended legislation: others would have countered the ill effects of pauperism on the economy by a deliberate check on the increase of the country's population by either birth control or enforced emigration. The Commission possessed, too, the evidence which it had collected and the views of its own membership, particularly those of Senior and Chadwick, who prepared its report. Finally, the discussions during the preparation of the Bill, and the arguments inside and outside Parliament, served to emphasise the variety of the views held on the subject of pauper treatment. The true understanding of the background against which the Boards of Guardians began their work rests, therefore, on an appreciation of the significance of much that had happened and much that had been said, before the first entries in their minute books were made.

The Boards of Guardians

The Boards of Guardians, for whose constitution the Poor Law Amendment Act made provision, continued to exist until the implementation of the Local Government Act of 1929. Parishes were joined together in convenient groups, and in each parish a Guardian was elected by all the inhabitants assessed to the poor rate, the number of votes to which individual parishioners were entitled being determined by the amount they were required to contribute.

Each Board of Guardians was directly responsible to the Poor Law Commissioners (replaced in 1847 by the Poor Law Board and in 1871 by the Local Government Board) for the administration for relief purposes of the group of parishes, all of which were to send their impotent poor to a central union workhouse, and whose overseers were stripped of almost all but emergency executive power. Each union had its own relieving officers, to whom the overseers were responsible, and who enquired into and assessed every application for relief; these officers could order assistance in kind or money to poor people in temporary difficulties, but were responsible to the Board for the expenses they incurred; anyone permanently incapable of supporting himself or his family was ordered into the workhouse. Medical officers, a master and mistress of the workhouse, and schoolteachers for pauper children, were employed under contract, on a union and not a parish basis, and all were answerable to the Guardians. The Guardians in their turn were subject to strict supervision from the central authority, whence came a flood of orders, regulations and directives.

The Whereabouts of Guardians' Records

After the abolition of the Boards of Guardians the custody of their records devolved upon the county borough and county authorities who took over their duties. The minute books, where they survive for the whole period from 1835 to 1930, are usually very bulky and need considerable storage space, which no doubt accounts for the fact that many have suffered from the poor physical conditions in which they have been kept, and others have been the victims of the salvage drives of the last war. Most local authorities who took over poor law administration have preserved a certain number of records, but these vary immensely in quantity and value, and the intending student should make doubly sure that adequate documentation exists before undertaking any piece of research on the work of the Guardians.

The Use of the Guardians' Minute Books

Like most official records, Guardians' Minute Books contain many purely formal entries, which are largely uninformative to the student. Indeed, the amount of detail contained in the volumes varies considerably from union to union, some being virtually useless as social documents, and others providing a wealth of information; it is probably true to say that the notes of the Guardians in the pre 1834 'Gilbert Unions' are the most valuable, as these boards were responsible only to the county justices, and little of their work was circumscribed by the regulations of a superior authority; consequently both matters of policy and individual actions are recorded at length; it is unfortunate that many of these records perished when the unions were reformed under the 1834 Act.

Much economic material can be obtained from the more informative minute books. Food prices are listed at length in tenders by various firms for supplying the workhouse; the relieving officers' reports on cases show the financial level at which many families lived, and analyses of cases show the incidence of sickness, the size of families and the accommodation thought adequate for the average labourer, both in the new industrial towns and the rural areas. The medical officers' reports can also be valuable, especially where details of treatment appear; there was usually more than one doctor under contract to each union, but one senior officer was in charge of the workhouse hospital, and supervised the work of the (usually, in the early days, untrained) nurses. The workhouse schools, although they catered for only a very small section of the community, were the first homes of compulsory state education; the reports of the schoolmaster or mistress, where these appear, can therefore provide interesting information for the student of educational history.

The minute books often contain contracts and specifications for the building of new union workhouses, or the alteration of old parish poorhouses; descriptions of the original state of the latter may also appear. Reports from the master

Guardians' Minute Books

show the day-today administration of the workhouse — the work the paupers were expected to do, the conditions under which they lived and the food they ate.

Reports of sub-committees sometimes appear in the minute books, and these provide more detailed information of various aspects of the work of the Boards, for example, the care of pauper children and of lunatics and the supervision of the administration of the workhouse. The Guardians were, from the beginning, regarded as authoritative bodies from whom local information could be obtained by the central government on a large variety of subjects not directly connected with poor relief. For example, at the end of 1836 the Constabulary Commissioners asked the Guardians for statistics bearing on the prevalence of crime and the methods employed to deal with it. Subsequent legislation invested the Guardians with other duties, among them the supervision of registration of births, deaths and marriages, of rating and assessment, of sanitation and, after the Elementary Education Act of 1876, of school attendance. The reports of committees dealing with these matters are sometimes found in the minutes, and many passing references to them, of course, occur.

The minute books of the Guardians are most valuable when used in conjunction with other surviving records of the unions — orders from the Poor Law Boards, workhouse day books, admission registers, letter books of the clerk to the guardians, and many other types of document. The reports and orders of the central authority, particularly those of the Poor Law Commissioners, will also prove valuable to the student, and these, of course, have not suffered from the depredations of time as have the local records. The private papers of the more influential Guardians may also serve to illumine the decisions made by the Boards, and the lists of Guardians, with the names of the parishes which they represented, found in the minute books will give the student an idea where to look for these. The problems of large towns and industry are also illuminated by the Guardians' minutes, a complete series of which can show clearly the gradual emergence of a new attitude to the poor and unfortunate. To the inhabitant of the Welfare State the workhouses seem grim places, but many of the Guardians were, even in the early period, genuinely concerned with the welfare of their pauper charges, and continually tried to improve conditions. The progress of poor law administration and the development of the social services during the period of the unions' authority is a very worthwhile subject for research.

Bibliography

Webb, S and **B**, *English Poor Law History*, (2 vols, 1927-9)
These volumes, in the Webbs' 'English Local Government' series, are the basic and indispensable works for the history of the period and of the old poor law.
Ashcroft, P F and **Preston, Thomas A**, *The English Poor Law System* (1888)
Cuttle, G, *The Legacy of the Rural Guardians* (1934)
The present writer's catalogue of Sussex Poor Law Records (1960) contains a fuller bibliography and a basic introduction to the English poor law which may be of assistance to students.

Chantry Certificates

Lawrence S Snell

[The Chantry Certificate for Week St. Mary, Cornwall, P.R.O. E. 301/15/73]

SAYNT MARYE WEKE. The chauntrye called Dame Percyvalles Chauntrye ffounded by Dame Percyvall to ffynde a pryste for ever not only to praye for her sowle within the paroche churche of Saynt Marye Weke aforesayd But also that he the sayd pryste do teache children freelye in a Scole founded by the said Dame Percyvall not farr distant from the sayd parishe churche And he to perceyve [sic] for his yerelye stipend or salarye xij^li· vj^s· to be levyed of the landes gyven amonge other uses to that entent and purpose. To ffynde a mancyple also to instruct and teache children under the sayd Scolemayster And he to have for the mayntenaunce of his lyving yerelye xxvj^s· viij^d·. To gyve to A laundresse to wasshe the clothes of the aforesayde Scolemaystre and Mancyple for her rewarde yerelye xiij^s· iiij^d·. And the Remayne of the sayd landes thabovenamyd ffoundresse wylled (all charges of reparacons aswell of the tenements and houses As also of the chalys and ornamentes belonging to the sayd chauntrye being firste susteyned and allowed) shulde be expendyd in the keping of an obytt yerelye for herr within the paryche churshe aforsayde.

The yerelye value of all the landes and possessyons belonging or appertaynyng to the chauntrye aforesayde — xv^li· xiiij^s· viij^d· wherof — Defalked — ffor rente resolute yerelye going owt of the sayd landes to dyverse and sondrye parsons xxj^s· vij^d· ffor the yerelye stipends of Wylliam Chalwell now Incumbent and Scolemayster there xij^li· vj^s· ffor the yerelye salarye of — now the mancyple there xxj^s· viij^d· ffot the rewards of the laundresse by the yere xiij^s· iiij^d· (Total) xv^li· viij^s· vij^d·. And so remayn clere the x^ths in this value not reprysed vij^s· j^d· whyche the sayd ffoundress wylled to be expendyd yerelye in the celebratyng of an obytt As is before declared.

The value of all the ornamentes, Jewelles, plate, goodes, catalles belonging or appertaynyng to the sayd Chauntrye ffounded by the abovenamyd Dame Percyvall As by a particular Inventorye therof made at large and redye to be shewed more playnlye maye appere — xxxvij^s·

Memorandum that ye sayd chauntrye is a great comfort to all ye countre there for yt they yt lyst may sett their children to borde there and have them tawght freely, for ye which purpose there is an house and officers appointed by ye ffoundacon accordynglye.

Chantry Certificates

The dissolution of the monasteries in 1536-9 and the confiscation of their wealth still left untouched considerable ecclesiastical property in the form of endowments of colleges, chantries, hospitals, brotherhoods and guilds. The Chantries Act of 1545 (37 Hen. VIII, c.4.) gave Henry VIII authority to dissolve these foundations and when he died in 1547 the work of suppression was carried on by his son, Edward VI, under the Chantries Act Of 1547 (1 Edw. VI, c.14). The results of the surveys carried out under these Acts are given in the Chantry Certificates. The type of information to be extracted from them can be seen from the column headings of the 1546 certificates which are as follows:

(i)   The number and names of all the chantries, hospitals, colleges, free-chapels, fraternities, brotherhoods, guilds and stipendiary priests.

41

Chantry Certificates

(ii) To what intents, purposes and deeds of charity they were founded, ordained and made, how far distant they were from the parish church, with the name of the parish in which any such chantry, college, etc. was founded, with the number of houseling people (communicants) within any such parish.

(iii) The yearly value of all the lands and possessions, temporal and spiritual, appertaining or belonging to them with the yearly deductions and resolutions going out of the same.

(iv) The value of all ornaments, jewels, plate, goods and chattels appertaining or belonging to any of the said chantries, hospitals, etc. yet undissolved.

(v) How many chantries, hospitals, colleges, etc. since the 4th day of February in the 27th year of the king's reign have been dissolved or obtained by any person without the king's licence, with the clear yearly value of the possessions thereof and the value of the goods and chattels of the same. Similar information is supplied in the Edwardian certificates which also often give a recommended pension for those chantry priests and their dependents, like the maniciple and the laundress above, when the chantry is dissolved.

From the 1546 chantry certificate from St. Mary Week, Cornwall, given above we see that the founder was Dame Percyvall (the later Edwardian Chantry certificate adds that she was Dame Thomasyn Percyvall, wife of Sir John Percyvall, knight and alderman, whom we know to have been Lord Mayor of London in 1498-9). We see that the object of the chantry foundation was to pray for her soul and to found a school near the parish church, that the chantry priest with a salary of £12.6s.0d. was to be the schoolmaster and that he was to be helped by a maniciple (wages 26/8d.) and a laundress (wages 13/4d.). The value of the lands is given as £15.4s.8d. out of which payments, rent resolute, stipends — were to be made to the value of £15.8s.7d., leaving 7/1d. to endow an obit. The value of the plate, jewels, etc., is said to be 37/= and a recommendation is made that the school be allowed to continue. If we go to the Edwardian chantry certificate for the same parish we find the additional information that the chantry was at the altar of St. John the Baptist in the parish church of Our Lady of Week, that the maniciple's name was George Spry and that his wife was the laundress, that the chantry priest's age was 55 years and he is described as 'being a man well learned and a great setter forth of God's word'. Examination of chantry certificates from different parts of England will show that the form varies but the general content is much the same, as the commissioners, who varied from county to county, were required to provide the same information. It will also be noticed that although the certificates are commonly known as Chantry Certificates they do, in fact, deal with a wide variety of endowments and foundations which are briefly described below:

Chantries

In its simplest form a chantry is a mass celebrated at an altar for the wellbeing of the founder during his life-time and for the repose of his soul after death. By the end of the thirteenth century chantries had become the most popular form of religious endowment, and during the fourteenth century we find chantries endowed by royalty, the nobility, great ecclesiastics and wealthy merchants. Sometimes the endowment provided for the setting up of a new and special chapel, and sometimes the addition of a new chapel to an existing building. The majority of endowments, however, were for the recitation of masses at an altar already existing in a church, the particular altar being specified in the terms of the bequest. In chantry foundations of persons of rank and wealth, the endowment often provided for the establishment of an almshouse or hospital. Here were housed and maintained a number of poor men or bedesmen, to whom the chantry priest, who was usually master of the hospital, served as chaplain and distributed their allowances, fuel and clothing. Founders, like Dame Percyvall above, often provided for a small school to be attached to the chantry.

Chantries were also endowed by religious gilds which secured an altar in the parish church and provided an endowment for the purpose of paying a priest to say mass daily for the brethren and sisters of the gild living and departed. From about the middle of the fifteenth century onwards the wealthy trade and craft gilds also became active in establishing their own chapels with the necessary endowments. These chapels were generally attached to parish churches, particularly in those towns where gild membership would be considerable. The enlargement and maintenance of many town churches was to a great extent due to the munificence of these gilds and fraternities. This is often an important factor in writing the history of a parish church.

Colleges: Often in cathedrals and the greater town churches large numbers of chantry priests were occupied solely in reciting masses for the dead, and the bishops considered it advisable to incorporate such bodies of priests into colleges where they could live communally, rather than in lodgings scattered all over the town. This practice, begun by bishops and cathedral bodies, of establishing colleges of chantry priests was followed by lay benefactors.

Obits: Poorer persons who were not in a position to found and endow a chantry left money for obits — the saying of mass for the repose of the soul annually on the anniversary of death; or for a place on a Beadroll, the list of persons prayed for on stated occasions. These privileges could be secured for a very small endowment producing sums from sixpence upwards. A slightly larger endowment would ensure the recitation of masses on the first, third, seventh and thirtieth days after the death of a testator, with an obit once a year.

Lights: Many parishes had small endowments, varying from a few pence to a few shillings, arising from lands, sheep, cattle which had been given to provide lights and lamps to set before the rood, the blessed Sacrament, or before images at side altars, symbolic of the ceaseless prayer offered through Christ or the saints. The Chantry certificates for Oxfordshire and Bedfordshire, for example, contain many references to these small endowments for obits and lights.

Location

Most of the extant chantry certificates are to be found in the Public Record Office in London. Details are to be found in a MS. Calendar entitled 'List of

Chantry Certificates

Exchequer Augmentations Office Certificates of Colleges and Chantries. E301'. This calendar contains references to chantries, etc., in Bedfordshire, Berkshire, Buckinghamshire, Cambridgeshire, Chester, Cornwall, Cumberland, Derby, Devon, Dorset, Durham, Essex, Gloucestershire, Hampshire, Herefordshire, Hertfordshire, Kent, Lancashire, Leicestershire, Lincolnshire, Middlesex, Norfolk, Northampton, Northumberland, Nottinghamshire, Oxfordshire, Rutland, Shropshire, Staffordshire, Suffolk, Surrey, Sussex, Warwickshire, Westmorland, Wiltshire, Worcestershire, Yorkshire. Wales — Anglesey, Brecknockshire, Cardiganshire, Carmarthenshire, Carnarvonshire, Denbighshire, Flintshire, Glamorganshire, Merioneth, Monmouth, Montgomeryshire, Pembrokeshire, Radnorshire.

A glance at this calendar will show that some counties have many Chantry Certificates extant, others very few. A further typescript list of miscellaneous documents concerned with the above counties is added at the end of the MS. Calendar and this list also contains references to chantries in Jersey and London.

Bibliography

Bond, F, *An Introduction to English Church Architecture from the 11th to 16th Centuries,* 1, (1913), 102-12.

Brown, J E, *Bedfordshire Chantry Certificates,* Bedford Arts Club.

Cook, G H, *Medieval Chantries and Chantry Chapels,* (1947).

Cotton, C, *Canterbury and Neighbourhood,* supp. to *Kent Chantries,* Kent Rec., xii, supp.

Cozens-Hardy, B, *Chantries in the Duchy of Lancaster in Norfolk, 1548,* Norfolk Arch., xxix, (1946), 201-10.

Graham, Rose, *Oxfordshire Chantry Certs,* Alcuin Club, (1920)

Green, E, *Somerset Chantry Certs.* Som. Rec. Soc., ii, (1888)

Hamilton, A, 'Shropshire Chantry Certs.' *Shropshire Arch. and Nat. Hist. Soc. Trans.,* 3rd ser., X, (1910), 269-392

Hussey, A, *Kent Chantry Certs.* Kent Arch. Soc. Rec. Branch, xii, (1935)

Maclean, Sir J, 'Gloucester Chantry Certs.' *Trans. Bristol and Glos. Arch. Soc,* viii, (1883-4), 229-308

Page, Sir W, *York Chantry Certs.* 2 vols. Surtees Soc-, xci, xcii, (1894-5)

Raines, F R, *A History of Chantries within the County Palatine of Lancaster,* Chetham Soc., lix and lx, (1862)

Ray, J E, *Sussex Chantry Records* Sussex Rec. Soc., xxxvi, (1931)

Rock, D, *The Church of Our Fathers,* iii (Pt 1; 1852), pp 104-40

Snell, L S, *Chantry Certs. for Cornwall,* Exeter, (1953)

Snell, L S, *Chantry Certs. for Devon and City of Exeter,* Exeter, (1961)

Thomson, A Hamilton, *The Certificates of the Chantry Commissioners for the College of Southwell in 1546 and 1548,* ThorotonSoc.,xv, 1912, pp.63-158; *The Chantry Cert. Rolls for the County of Nottingham,* ib. Thoroton Soc., xvi, (1913) pp. 91-133, xvii, (1914), pp 59-119, xviii, 1915, pp 83-184

Thomson, A Hamilton, *The Historical Growth of the Parish Church,* (1911), ch. 2, pp 24-50.

Wood-Legh, K L, *Studies in Church Life under Edward III,* (1934), ch4, pp 89-126, with ref.

Hearth Tax Returns

Roger Howell

[Entries of hearth tax assessments for Binsey, Oxfordshire, from the Exchequer Duplicate for Oxfordshire, 1665, in the Public Record Office, E179/164/513; printed in Weinstock, see bibliography.)

James Ward	v
Thomas Crutch	ix
Thomas Prickett	vj
James Heron	ij
Henry Crutch	iij
Ann Heron widdow	iij
Richard Heron sen.	i
	xxix

William Magger	ij }	discharged by
John Rannce	ij }	poverty
	iiij	

Hearth Tax

At the Restoration, the Convention Parliament calculated that Charles II would be able to discharge the ordinary expenses of peacetime government with an income of £1,200,000 a year. The failure of the financial settlement to produce this amount led to the need for supplementary taxation, one form of which was the Hearth Money. The Act of 1662 [I4 Car. II, c. 10] which established the tax created an annual due of 2s. for every hearth, to be collected half-yearly by the petty constables, high constables and sheriffs unless the occupant was exempted on the grounds of poverty. Exemptions were made for those whose poverty already excused them from paying poor and church rates or whose house was worth less than 20s. per annum or who could prove that neither they, nor any other person using the same, occupied land of 20s. value or possessed property to the value of £10. Inmates of hospitals and almshouses were also exempted, as were private ovens, kilns, etc. The 1662 act was twice modified. In 1663 [15 Car. II, c.13] new checks were introduced at each stage of the assessment and collection on the grounds that the local officers had been negligent in their duties, and all hearths, whether taxable or not, were to be indicated in the returns. In 1664 [16 Car. II, c. 3] the responsibility for them was transferred to a newly created set of officials, the chimney men.

The tax met with immediate opposition, and the levying was hampered by concealment of hearths and the unwillingness of local officials to cooperate with the chimney men. In 1666 a contract for farming the tax for seven years was completed, an experiment which proved to have little success, the farm

Short Guides to Records 7

being surrendered in November 1668. The tax was later farmed out more successfully in 1674 and 1675. At the conclusion of the last farm in 1684, the tax was put into commission and so remained until it was abolished in 1688.

Location of Hearth Tax Records and their Format

Hearth tax records are to be found either among the county records or in the Public Record Office. The documents are of several types. A copy of the assessment which was enrolled at the Quarter Sessions in the area of collection has survived in a few counties only among the County Quarter Sessions records, and such texts are useful for supplementing (and on occasion replacing completely) records which are damaged or lost among the central archives. The bulk of the hearth tax material is to be found in the P.R.O. and can be loosely characterised as falling into six groups of records as Meekings suggests. In the first place, there are accounts recording the payments from the collection areas. Secondly, there are the Exchequer duplicates of the assessments. Although the latter are extremely bulky, they are more satisfactory as a rule than the local records, being more formal and legible than the parish constables' returns to the Quarter Sessions. The other four groups contain schedules of arrears of payments, particulars of accounts, the record of the Exchequer tallies of receipt, and the auditors' miscellanea.

In many ways, the most useful of these records are the assessments, comprising lists of names and numbers of hearths. The 1662 assessment contains only the names of those with chargeable hearths, while the returns made under the revising act of 1663 (of which the first are for the half year ending Lady Day, 1664) contain lists of persons chargeable and not chargeable, usually arranged in parallel columns. Both assessments may have the names of the petty constables after each parish or division. The lists of names which the farmers of the tax kept were retained among their own private business books and were not returnable to the Exchequer, so that the P.R.O. does not contain hearth tax assessments and returns of every date from 1662 to 1689.

The Uses of Hearth Tax Records

For the local historian, and particularly for the genealogist, hearth tax records are an invaluable guide to the people resident within each parish or hamlet. Although somewhat vitiated through widespread evasion, they do give a record of nearly every family, however humble. The Essex hearth tax of 1662 lists about 20,000 names excluding paupers, while that of 1671 lists about 25,000 names including paupers; the Suffolk hearth tax of 1674 lists about 28,400 names. Beyond this, their use for biographical research is limited. As the illustration shows, they provide no information other than a list of names assessed with the number of hearths. There are no indications of the occupation of the householder, except that smiths and bakers may be identified by the mention of a forge or oven. On occasion, some indication of the householder's status may be given by the addition of a title such as Esq., Gent., Clerk, widow, but the practice is not uniform. The 1665 return for

Oxfordshire, for example, is striking in its lack of mention of parish clergy, although the title Doctor or Clerk occasionally appears. The records of the diocese reveal that a number of men listed without any identifying mark were the incumbents of parishes.

The hearth tax returns, incomplete as they may be, provide one source for the population of England in this period. Although they cannot be used to obtain any completely accurate figures for the population of a given area, they can be used at least to provide some indication of the relative size of various areas. An analysis of the returns can, for example, give some idea of the population distribution and the relative density of population in various parts of a county. Within obvious limitations, they can also be used to estimate population. The main problem here is that of deciding what multiplier to use in order to convert the number of households or the number of hearths into the number of people. There is no generally accepted figure for the size of the average household, and, indeed, it is likely that the size of households varied considerably with the location of the dwelling and with the degree of urbanisation of the area in which it was located. Pickard has suggested that a figure as large as 6-8 should be taken as the multiplier, but it would probably be safer not to assume a higher average per household than 4.5 to 5. In Exeter, investigation of the records of the Orphans' Court revealed an average of 4.3 children per family, which would, of course, result in a multiplier of 6.3 (W. T. MacCaffrey, *Exeter 1540-1640: The Growth of an English Country Town*, Cambridge, Mass., 1958, p 12). Over the whole kingdom, the average would seem to be somewhat lower. Gregory King, whose general reliability has become more widely accepted (see D. C. Coleman, 'Labour in the English Economy of the Seventeenth Century', *Economic History Review*, 2nd Series, vol. viii, 1956, p 283 and the authorities cited there), made a provisional allotment of persons to houses on the basis of the different number of hearths the houses contained, with figures varying from 3.7 for a single hearth to 30 for over twenty hearths. It is possible to get very nearly the same results as would be reached by using his elaborate calculations with individual hearths by multiplying the total entries of hearths by 4.5. Certainly the bulk of the information available, most of it unfortunately from later periods, would suggest the use of the smaller multiplier 4.5 rather than the larger one of 6 or above. Some further revision of the final figure upwards is necessary to account for servants.

The returns also yield some information about the distribution of wealth and poverty within a given area. It is generally sound to assume that the more hearths a house had, the wealthier the inhabitant was unless it can be demonstrated positively that the house was in joint occupation. Classifying the houses in groups determined by the number of hearths, one can to some extent see the pattern of wealth or poverty. The most useful groupings are houses with a single hearth, those with two, those with three to five, those with six to nine, and those with ten or more. A total of less than three hearths usually indicates an economic situation below the comfortable level, while a total of more than ten would indicate considerable affluence. It is also useful to arrange the material by average number of hearths, since this may reveal information about the settlement pattern, particularly in an urban area. Hoskins' analysis of Exeter made in this fashion revealed clearly that the wealth of the town was concentrated in the central nucleus, while the poorer areas were pressed to the outside against the town limits. In Newcastle-upon-Tyne, where the same pattern is repeated, there was a significant correlation between the areas with a high average number of hearths and the areas which returned most of the members of the two branches of the town government, the aldermen and the Twenty-Four.

Bibliography

A number of hearth tax assessments have been printed. For a list, see West. Those that are mentioned here have useful commentary. Hoskins' book contains an analysis of wealth and poverty based on the returns.

Dowell, S, *A History of Taxation and Taxes in England from the Earliest Times to the Present Day* (London, 4 vols, 1884)

Emmison, F G and **Gray, I,** *County Records* (Hist. Ass. pamphlet S3, 1948), pp. 15, 28-32, lists surviving hearth tax assessments in local custody (inf. not reported in rev. edn., 1961

Hoskins, W G, *Industry, Trade, and People in Exeter, 1688-1800* (Manchester, 1935)

Little, B, *The City and County of Bristol, A Study in Atlantic Civilization* (London, 1954), appendix 1

Marshall, L M, 'The Levying of the Hearth Tax, 1662-1688', *EHR,* vol. li (1936)

Marshall, L M, *The Rural Population of Bedfordshire, 1671 to 1921,* Publications of the Bedfordshire Historical Record Society, vol. xvi (Bedford, 1934)

Meekings, C A F (ed), *Dorset Hearth Tax Assessments 1662-4* (Dorchester, 1951)

Meekings, C A F (ed), *Surrey Hearth Tax, 1664, Being an Alphabetical List of Entries in the Record* Surrey Record Society, vol. xvii (London, 1940)

Pickard, R, *The Population and Epidemics of Exeter in Pre-Census Times* (Exeter, 1947)

Powell, E, 'The Hearth Taxes for the Town of Cambridge, A.D. 1664 and 1674', *Cambridge Antiquarian Society Proceedings and Communications,* vol. xx (1915), pp. 80-95

Victoria County History, *Cambridgeshire,* v.3, pp 500-4; v.4, pp272-80.

VCH, *Essex,* v.4 pp303-10. *Leicestershire* v.4, pp 156-9. *City of York,* pp 162-5

Weinstock, M M B (ed), *Hearth Tax Returns, Oxfordshire, 1665,* Oxfordshire Record Society, vol. 21 (Oxford, 1940)

Welford, R, 'Newcastle Householders in 1665: Assessment of Hearth or Chimney Tax', *Archaeologia Aeliana* 3rd Series, vol. vii (1910), pp. 49-76

West, J, *Village Records* (London, 1962)

Episcopal Visitation Books

Dorothy M Owen

[From Ely Diocesan Records B/2/11, f. 101 Liber actorum in vis']

Die veneris quints die mensis march anno domini iuxta computacionem ecclesie Anglicane 1590 in ecclesia parochiali beate Marie maioris iuxta forum ville Cant.' coram magistro Willelmo Revell surrogato

Harston

Thomas Tucke	Notatur for that he was at the foteball in the tyme of eveninge prayer upon sondaye last. Quibus etc. dominos duxit dictum T.T. diligenter perquisisit' latitan' et non,
viis et modis	invent' nec comparent' citand' fore viis et modis in XII diem marcii pred' quo die exhibito dicto decreto et executo' etc. comparuit dictus T. et affirmavit that he was then in the Campinge Close but did not playe, deinde dominus iniunxit ei con fess'
confes'	monuitque cum ad purg' eundem prout in schedula et cum certif'inde XIX marcii pred' quo die comparuit dictus T. quem dom, monuit ad idem prox. viz. XXVI
suspen'	marcii pred', quando non comparuit dom. pronunc' eum contumac' et in pena etc. eum ab ingressu ecclesie suspend'. Emanavit.

Friday 5th March 1590/1 in St. Mary the Great next the Market at Cambridge before Mr. William Revell, surrogate.

Harston   T. T. presented — at which time and place (a citation understood) T. T. lying hid and not found when sought and not appearing, the judge ordered him to be cited *viis et modis*, by any possible means, for 12th March aforesaid. On this day the citation and certificate of its execution being exhibited, the said T. appeared and affirmed The judge then enjoined him to confess the fault as it appeared in the presentment and ordered him to bring in a certificate that he had confessed on 19th March. T. appeared on this day and was told to come on the next court day, 26th March. When he did not appear on that day the judge pronounced him contumacious and suspended him from entry to the church. A decree of suspension was issued.

Nature of Visitation

Visitation of his diocese by a bishop became customary in the thirteenth century. He and his officials gradually evolved a machinery for the visitation and correction of the secular clergy and the laity and the enforcement of the canon law. This machinery was inherited by the bishops of the reformed church who so modified and extended it, especially in its corrective aspects, that it became a powerful instrument for the maintenance of the Elizabethan religious settlement. In 1603 canons CIX and CXIX standardised and codified visitation practices and for the next century at least visitation continued to be an important element in the life of the church. It was customary for the bishop to hold his primary visitation during the first year after his enthronement and thereafter to repeat his visitation at three (or sometimes four) yearly intervals. The visitation was held in a few large centres which could conveniently be reached from the surrounding parishes, generally by the bishop's principal legal official, the chancellor, or in larger dioceses, by a *commissary* deputed to visit a single archdeaconry. These officials subsequently held further sessions, usually in the diocesan centre, to complete the business of the visitation.

From the fifteenth century it had been customary for visitors to require from the churchwardens or other laymen in the parish, at each visitation, a *presentment* of things wrong in the parish and the Elizabethan bishops, seeking to use this system efficiently, had begun to issue *articles of enquiry* to guide the churchwardens in their presentments. Meanwhile a *general monition* was sent out, to be read in each parish church, summoning 'all parsons and vicars to exhibit their letters of orders, certificates of subscription to the articles and licences and dispensations, all preachers and lecturers, curates, schoolmasters and ushers to exhibit licences, all churchwardens and sidesmen to take their oaths and make the presentments, executors to bring in wills and all criminals and delinquents to answer articles'. From the churchwardens' replies to the articles, which are often known as *detecta* (things uncovered), a *citation* or summons was prepared for those needing correction; if a parish had a large number of such people a collective citation naming them all (*quorum nominal*) was served by the *apparitor* or court official who certified its service to the visitor. If those cited failed to appear a further citation, to be served by any possible means (*viis et modis*), was issued and disobedience to this involved the penalty of *suspension* from entry to the church.

The diocesan officials prepared two books for use at the visitation, with the names of the parishes arranged under the headings of the rural deaneries. These were a *liber cleri, call book* or *exhibit book* containing the names of the clergy, churchwardens and schoolmasters summoned to the visitation to exhibit and a *liber compertorum* (things found out) which had copies of all the more important presentments. In some cases the comperta were so arranged that space was left to record the various stages in the correction of the crime but at other times a separate book, including the comperta but chronologically arranged and known as an *act book* (*liber actorum*), was made for this purpose. All of these books may be called visitation books and at some periods, in some dioceses, they have been bound together. No diocese seems to have been consistent in its practice about the recording of visitations; some form of call book is usually found but both comperta and act books appear at different times each yielding much the same sort of information.

Location of Records

It is reasonable to say that the ancient dioceses have among their records a certain number of all the types of visitation books of the sixteenth and seventeenth centuries and that the large semi-independent archdeaconries of the old dioceses of Lincoln, London and Norwich have often retained the records of their visitation by commissaries. Mr. Welch's pamphlet on *Ecclesiastical Records* will treat the subject of location and accessibility of these records more fully and, meanwhile, where information cannot easily be obtained, application may be made to the registrar of the National Register of Archives (Miss W. D. Coates), Quality House, Quality Court, W.C.2.

Uses of the Records

The articles on which presentments are based are concerned with breaches of the canon law but pressure from the government or the visitor's own sympathies may cause at different times the inclusion of further questions, about recusants, puritanical practices or charitable endowments, and the visitation books are invaluable aids to the study of the enforcement of conformity. There remain the basic recurring articles which concern:

1. the fabric of the church and the chancel and the state of the churchyard
2. the furniture and fittings of the church
3. the buildings of the glebe, including the parsonage house
4. the parochial clergy and holders of episcopal licences, schoolmasters, surgeons and midwives
5. churchwardens and other parish officials
6 the laity; canon CIX said that those to be presented were those guilty of adultery, whoredom, incest, drunkenness, swearing, ribaldry and usury, schismatics, disturbers of the divine service and those refusing to communicate at Easter.

The summaries of replies to these articles are usually written in English in a clear and legible hand; even in the act books it is not difficult to find and read the entries relating to a particular village and the local historian will find many interesting details about his parish history. The presentments and the replies of those accused appear always to quote authentic speech: in 1473 the churchwardens of Linwood (Lincolnshire) said

> 'Thyrston Fayrclough has off the kirke goodys XXVIs. VIIId. And has had many yerys And They chan nevoyr get yt owt off hys handys and God knowes they have gret nede therto for renewynge of ther belles'.

Replies to queries about the state of the church and the parsonage house have much detailed information about roofs, windows, walls, and steeples. It is often possible to discover the dates of restorations or of additions to the fabric and to assess the damage done during the Civil War and Commonwealth. Those interested in church plate and bells will find a good deal of information, partly negative it is true, and presentments about church books and furnishings occasionally give clues to the religious state of the neighbourhood. In 1638, for example, the churchwardens of St. Paul's Lincoln said 'the parish is so poore that we are not able to procure Jewell's works and Erasmus' paraphrases because they are so deare and not used in anye parishe churche in this city'.

Episcopal Visitation Books

The visitation books often illuminate, if obliquely, the character, education, religious views and status of the clergy: a vicar of Baston (Lincolnshire) was accused in 1473, for example, of wasting time in playing with laymen a game of hand-ball called 'le tenys'. Those interested in educational and medical history can collect biographical data and light on the state of the profession: at Grantham in 1588 one Augustine 'a Scote borne' who seemed to be practising unlicensed proved to be a doctor of medicine. A midwife in 1594 told women in labour to invoke the name of the Lady Mary, and Agnes Robson of Oundle in 1538 cured sick pigs with a charm. Allegations of witchcraft were made throughout the sixteenth and seventeenth centuries but the attack on May games, Midsummer revels and other survivals of pagan festivals seems to have been peculiar to the reign of Elizabeth. It most often occurs in charges of sabbath breaking and absence from church: in 1591 John Loughtes, a minstrel, was presented for 'pipeinge or playinge before the morice dauncers at Sawston (Cambridgeshire) upon Trinitys Sondaye and twoe Sondayes before midsomer daye, beinge then absent from his parishe churche'.

The names of non-conforming ministers, Sabbath breakers, abstainers from communion and 'schismatics' are valuable in any study of recusancy, puritanism and early nonconformity. In the eastern dioceses of Lincoln and Norwich and the archdeaconry of Nottingham they often include the future leaders of the Puritan emigrations to America. The Sabbath breakers also help to illuminate the economic and social life of the parish: they use Sunday to thresh beans, cart manure, and reap corn, they play football and frequent Reach fair. Richard Curde of March, a fen dweller, 'did go a gatheringe wilde fowle eggs and once he did yoke a horse and drawe a boate upon a sled'.

So much for the accusations, which are straightforward, easily read and in English. The prosecutions, much abbreviated, in Latin, hastily written, are less accessible and Mr. Williams decided to omit them from his edition of a visitation book. Some help can be got in deciphering them, for Mr. Brinkworth explains many of the abbreviations and phrases in the introductions to the two texts he has edited and Canon Jenkins translated a number of them, giving the original Latin in the footnotes. With this help the policy of the ecclesiastical authorities towards criminals, the fate of those accused of recusancy and the excuses of the Sunday footballer may all be discovered.

Bibliography

Brinkworth, E R C, *Episcopal Visitation Book for the Archdeaconry of Buckingham* (Bucks. Record Society, vol. 7, 1947)

Brinkworth, E R C, *The Archdeacon's Court: Liber actorum, 1584* (Oxfordshire Record Society, vols. 23 and 24, 1942, 1946) *Act Book*

Burn Richard, *Ecclesiastical Law* (London, 2 vols, 1763), article, Visitation

Gibson, Edmund, *Codex Iuris Ecclesiastici Anglicani* (London, 1713) title XLII, Visitation general and parochial

Hamilton, Thompson A, *Visitation in the Diocese of Lincoln 1517-31* (Lincoln Record Society vol. 33, 1940) *Comperta and Proceedings*

Episcopal Visitation Books

Jenkins, Claude, 'Act Book of the Archdeaconry of Taunton' in *Collectanea 11,* **Palmer, T F** (ed), (Somerset Record Society, vol 43, 1928, *Act Book*

Johnstone, Hilda, *Churchwardens Presentments 17th Century* (Sussex Record Society, vols 49-50, 1949-5). *Comperta only*

Kennedy, W P M and **Frere W H**, *Elizabethan Episcopal Administration* vol. 1, (Alcuin Club, vol. 25, 1924) an important discussion of visitation articles

Midgley, L M, *Survey of Ecclesiastical Archives*, (Pilgrim Trust, typescript, 1951), Copies of this work can be seen at the British Museum, Lambeth Palace Library, Bodleian Library and University Library, Cambridge

Williams, J F, *Bishop Redman's Visitation 1597* (Norfolk Record Society, vol. l8, 1946), *Comperta and proceedings,* latter omitted

Estate Acts of Parliament

Maurice Bond OBE

On 15 March 1717 Richard Heath, a boy of eleven, of East Clandon, Surrey, petitioned the House of Lords for leave for a Bill to vest in trustees the estates he had inherited the previous November from his late father, Sir Thomas Heath, in order to pay his father's debts. On 6 May the Bill was read a first time. It was enacted six weeks later, on 22 June, thereafter appearing in the printed lists as 3 George I, chapter 12 (Private). The text of this Act, preserved in the House of Lords Record Office, opens by describing the Heath estates and the deeds relating to their tenure; it then recites the many incumbrances on the estate, including such items as:

'to Henry Quennell Butcher by Bond dated the Eighth day of September 1715 in the penalty of £560 for payment of £280 on the Ninth day of December then next following And to Thomas Martin yeoman by another Bond dated the Twenty third day of Aprill 1715 in the penalty of £200 for payment of £102. 10s. on the Twenty fourth day of October then next following. . . .'

[After the full record of Sir Thomas Heath's indebtedness, amounting in all to £6000, the Act continues:]

'And whereas the Personall Estate of the said Sir Thomas Heath is not sufficient to pay his Debts [Sir Thomas had left £1022 personal estate. The petition alleged that if the debts were not paid until Richard Heath came of age the mounting interest would cause them to exceed both his real and his personal estate.] ... be it ENACTED ... That the said Farms Lands Tenements and hereditaments called Burtleys Blackmore Heath Farme ... The said Mannor of East Clandon [etc.] are hereby vested in and setled upon Dame Dorothy Heath Relict ... Richard Heath Clarke and John Heath Gentleman their heires and Assignes In trust ... that they ... shall with all convenient speed absolutely sell and dispose of the said Lands [etc.] ... and then pay off and discharge the severall Mortgages [etc.]'

And so in just over three months this small country estate, foundering in debt, was rescued by Parliament. Under the provisions of the Act the Manor of East Clandon was conveyed to Sir Peter King — incidentally, one of two judges to whom the initial petition of Richard Heath had been referred by the Lords for an expert legal opinion, a future Lord Chancellor, and ancestor of the Earls of Lovelace. By this sale the Heath family fortunes were saved and the young Richard was able to continue to live in the family mansion of Hatchlands. A subsequent owner went bankrupt and also needed to be saved by an Estate Act, the Raymond Estate Act of 22 George III, *c.* 43 (Private).

Classes of Estate Act

History is written today not only from chronicles and other literary sources, but, to an ever-increasing extent, from records connected with legal processes.

Estate Acts of Parliament

For the social and economic historian especially, the whole complex of legal matters surrounding property and its tenure is basic. The class of records of which the Heath Estate Act is a good example therefore forms important source material for history, as useful as at first sight it appears complicated.

The series of Private legislative records of Parliament to regulate the tenure of property in the post-medieval period (with which we are alone concerned here) begins in 1512 and comes down to the present day. In all, the records deal with at least six different types of subject (see the list in the following paragraph), but well over a half of the long series relate, as did the example given above, to the settlement of estates. The need for Acts of this type arose from restrictions imposed on family estates which became increasingly rigorous in the course of the seventeenth century. By the 'strict settlement', as the most highly developed type of settlement was called, an estate was conveyed to the owner for life only, then to his son for life, with remainder in tail to the eldest grandson, and similar remainders to the other grandsons, trustees being named to protect the interests of these, as yet unborn, grandsons. The son, after inheriting, would very probably agree with *his* son to re-settle the property in a similar way, in the interest of yet another generation. The various reasons causing each generation in many families to continue to make strict settlements are set out in Habakkuk H J, 'Marriage Settlements in the Eighteenth Century', *Transactions of the Royal Historical Society*, 4th series, vol. xxxii (1950), pp. 17-20 and Mingay G E, *English Landed Society in the Eighteenth Century* (1963), pp. 34-5. See also Thompson F M L, *English Landed Society in the Nineteenth Century* (1963), pp. 64-7, 214, 229-31, 319. Thus sale normally would be impossible, unless the life tenant and his son (after he had attained his majority and before another settlement had been made) decided jointly to bar the entail. In the mid- eighteenth century perhaps one-half of the land of England was held in this way, and by 1848 it was estimated that the proportion had even increased to about two-thirds. The system clearly met at least some contemporary needs. In particular it prevented reckless and dissolute heirs from squandering the whole of the family resources and it secured provision for widows, as well as for the children of intended marriages. There were, however, also grave disadvantages. It was difficult for the non-landed to buy their way into the ranks of gentry (which thus became increasingly stratified), and the landowners themselves suffered from inability to raise large sums of money for a sudden need, whether in order to pay off debts, or more importantly, to improve the management of the land or develop new uses, such as mining. The safety valve was a private Act of Parliament,that is, an Estate Act, and from 1660 onwards Estate Acts to alter settlements increased rapidly in number, eventually so impeding the other work of Parliament that between 1698 and 1706 a code of Standing Orders was worked out by the Lords 'to prevent the increase of Private Bills in Parliament: and the surprizing the House in their proceeding thereupon'. Estate legislation as a general class reached a climax during the reign of George III, when there were some 1672 Estate Acts in all, but the annual total remained an important annual total remained an important element in the legislative programme until the Settled Land Act of 1882 gave power to life-tenants to sell their land, and all but ended the long series of settlement Acts.

Settlement Acts were however but one sub-division of the class of Estate Act. Since the sixteenth century there have been five additional main categories. These may be listed briefly as follows (they are practically self-explanatory both in nature and in importance): (1) Acts to establish, incorporate, regulate, or vary the objects of charitable institutions. Schools and colleges bulk largely in this class, and the historian of education should therefore find source material here. (2) Acts to unite or disunite livings; to settle rights of presentation; to enable new churches to be built; to annex benefices to other objects. (These are relatively few in number.) (3) Acts to authorise the legally disabled to carry out their aims, e.g. to enable those under twenty-one to make marriage settlements, to buy and sell estates, and to grant leases. (4) A small but important class of Act enables boundaries of parishes to be ascertained or changed. (5) Finally, Acts may give power to appoint new trustees to bodies already set up by Act or to implement the purposes of private deeds and wills.

The Uses of Estate Act Records

The decisive and far-reaching character of an Act of Parliament clearly makes Acts and other records of legislation primary sources for historians. What here needs emphasis is the usefulness of Estate Acts in general and, particularly, the importance of the largest but all too little known class, that of settlement Acts. In these are to be found precise statements as to the tenure of property; manors, farms and fields with details of their areas and of their tenants being specified and, in later Acts, systematically tabulated in annexed schedules. Here is a useful fixed point for those studying family or local history: a survey guaranteed not only as a result of examination in the committees of the two houses, but also, after 1706, by a separate and annexed report from two judges in Westminster Hall. Topographical information is supplemented by much genealogical and personal detail. Family relationships are set out explicitly; dowries and jointures are summarised and their effect considered; and, as in our example above, the most elaborate statements are made detailing the financial situation of those concerned. This information, moreover, relates to a surprisingly wide social range, for it was not only the nobility or the wealthier gentry who sought Estate Acts: doctors, clergymen, business men and impoverished widows might also petition Parliament; the potential clientele of the Private Bill Offices of the two Houses was in fact as extensive as the ownership of property.

Analysis of Source Material

At this point it should be observed that the text of the final Act (important as that is) is not the only source available. All Estate Bills follow a quite intricate Parliamentary course, and from several of the fifteen stages in that process documents may survive. The general picture of Estate legislation is as follows:

HOUSE OF LORDS
1. Petition to the Lords to introduce Bill.
2. [1706 on] Reference to two Judges.
3. Report of Judges to House.
4. First Reading of Bill (formal).
5. Second Reading (usually formal).
6. Consideration in Select Committee.
7. Report to the House.
8. Third Reading.

HOUSE OF COMMONS
[Note: Frequently the stages in the Commons were brief or even formal]

9. First Reading.
10. Second Reading.
11. Consideration in Select Committee.
12. Report to the House.
13. Third Reading.

14. Consideration of Amendments (if any) made in one/both Houses by the other House.
15. Royal Assent in the Lords.

The Bill was usually (though not inevitably) introduced into the House of Lords first, and the bulk of the work was done by the Lords — a fortunate circumstance for students, as the Lords records survived the fire of 1834 at Westminster (the Commons records being largely destroyed), and all material so preserved can now be consulted in the House of Lords Record Office. In addition, however, much relevant material can be found locally. The texts of nearly all the Estate Acts passed in the nineteenth and twentieth centuries were printed and are available in the collected editions of Local and Private Acts in the larger libraries. In local Record Offices can often be found drafts of petitions, correspondence and other documents relating to the passage of the Bill. Quite frequently, printed texts are also found. These are somewhat deceptively entitled 'An Act', for these prints, when they are of pre-1800 date, are normally the texts not of the Act, but of the Bill, which were used during its passage through the two Houses. A complete analysis of the surviving material usually available for Estate Acts between 1512 and the present day is given on the next page.

The House of Lords Record Office

This brief account of a single type of Private Act and its associated records will, it is hoped, facilitate the use of an important range of Parliamentary source material. Estate Acts, however, form one only of some thirty-four classes of Private Act, and, in series with the records and printed sources described above, may be found very similar material relating to the other thirty-three classes, dealing with Bridges, Roads, Railways, Canals, Inclosures, Gas and Electricity services, Water supply, Fisheries and similar subjects, in addition to a long range of records concerned with Personal categories such as Divorce, Naturalisation and Change of Name. What has here been said about Estate Acts is to a varying extent applicable to the other thirty-three classes. A guide to the various types of record relating to transport is provided by the present writer in 'Materials for Transport History amongst the Records of Parliament', *Journal of Transport History* vol. iv (1959), pp. 37-52. All students,

Source	Manuscript	Print	Calendar
Petition to Lords [stage 1]	1592 on; in H[ouse of] L[ords] R[ecord] O[ffice]; often lengthy and very informative	Not printed	The whole of the surviving material for 1592–1714 is calendared in Appendices to the *Reports of the Historical Manuscripts Commission*, to 1693, and thereafter in *Manuscripts of the House of Lords* (New series) vols. i–xi. Each stage in the progress of each Bill is listed in the *Lords Journals* (1510–date) and *Commons Journals* (1547–date) and is clearly indexed in the relevant *Indexes* under the short title of the Bill. See also the two Indexes listed in the Bibliography below
Judges' Report [3]	1706 on; H.L.R.O. Useful for judgments on conflicting statements and claims	n.p.	
The Bill [4]	1592 on; H.L.R.O.	1720 on; prints may be in local R.O.; also in H.L.R.O. (see the comment in the text above)	
Lords Committee Proceedings [6]	H.L.R.O. These are usually quite brief. See also Witness and Trustee Acceptance Books	n.p.	
Commons Committee Proceedings [11]	1835 on; H.L.R.O.	n.p.	
Debates in the two Houses [7–14]	The Bills were seldom debated; what accounts exist are collected in Cobbett, *Parliamentary History* (to 1803) and in the subsequent Hansard, *Parliamentary Debates*		
The Act [15]	1512 on; H.L.R.O. The key text; sometimes of considerable length and complexity	From 1798 in *Local Acts*; after 1815 in *Private Acts*, though a few still not printed	

however, needing further information about any type of Parliamentary source material should write to the Clerk of the Records at the House of Lords, or, with due notice, call at the House of Lords Record Office, which is open to all members of the public throughout the year during specified office hours. Since 1946 this office has provided increased facilities for research, and, subject to the needs of Parliament itself, its staff are anxious to give all the help in their power to direct students towards the appropriate documentary and printed material there available.

Bibliography

The Calendar of House of Lords Manuscripts and other publications mentioned above, and:

Bond, N F, 'Acts of Parliament' in *Archives* vol. iii (1958), pp. 201-18, and published separately by the British Records Association.

Bramwell, George, *Analytical Table of the Private Statutes 1727-1812* (1813)

'List of Main Classes of Records', *House of Lords Record Office Memorandum* No. 1(E) (revised edition, 1963). This and the following Memorandum are available free on application to the Clerk of the Records, House of Lords

'Private Bill Records of the House of Lords', *House of Lords Record Office Memorandum* No. 16 (1957)

Index to Local and Personal Acts 1801-1947 (HMSO, 1949).

Wills

R Sharpe France

[The will of Matthew Becke of Manchester, Cheshire Rec. Office]

In Dei nomine Amen. The xxij th day of November in the yere off our Lord a m ccccc and xx I Mathew Beke wholle off mynd and syke in bodye, felyng perells of dethe, make my tastement in this maner

Inprimis I bequethe my sole to Almyghtie God and my bodye to be buried in the colledge church of Manchester, And in the name off my mortuarie a horse. I bequethe unto the roode seller off Manchestre when yt shalbe proceed xl^s. Item I bequethe to Wygan church xx^a. Item I bequethe unto litell Thomas Beke v^{li}. Item I bequethe unto Laurence Chetham xx^s to pray for my sawle. Item I bequethe to the mendyng of the payment in Salford lane Vj^{s}s Viij^d. Item I bequethe unto the mendyng off Newton lawne Vj^s Viij^d. Item I bequethe unto the mendyng off Dob lane vj^s Viij^d. Item it ys my will that a welle disposed priest shal syng and pray for my sowle a yere. Item I bequethe to Marion, George Brych wyff, my wyffes gyrdyll and both paire of bedes. Item I wille that the Marion have my wyves best downe and best kyrtill. Item I bequethe unto Sir Robert Bek my best gowne and my best blakk chamlett dublett and my best wolstyd dublett. Item I bequeth unto George Brych my second gowne and my tawny chamlett dowblett and a wolystyd dublett. Item I bequeth unto litill Thomas Beke my gawbardyne to make him a gowne. Item I bequeth to Merget Hadelande a kyrtyll. Item I bequeth to owr ladyes service in Manchestre ij^s. The residue off my goodes not bequetheyd I bequeth unto my brother Thomas Beke and Sir Robert Beke, whom I ordene myn executors to dyspose as the shall thynke best for my sowle helth, and Sir James Grene supervisor to see that this my last will be fulfilled att Manchester the day and yere aforsaid thes witnes, George Brych, Laurence Chetham. Sir James Grene and others.

[Codicil to the will of Thomas Clayton of Adlington, gentleman, 11 Aug. 1721, Lancs. Rec. Office WCW 1722]

After my death consider the day of burial, then let letters be writ and sent up and down to neighbours, friends and relations; provide a cold dinner for the better sort and set it in the little parlour, a cold dinner for the ordinary sort and set it in the hall. I would have a dole given to the poor of twopence apice. I would have no drinking at Standish town exceeding five shillings, a house for horses standing, twenty shillings in the whole. I would have eight excutcheons on my hearse and the coachman to have on the black coat being the same coat worn by the coachman at my wives burial, and give it to the coachman for his pains. I would have relations and gentlemen to have hatbands and gloves, and for mourning. I would have my son Richard Clayton, his wife and William Clayton my grandson to have twelve pounds to put them in mourning if William Clayton be in the country. My son-in-law Nicholas Rigby, his wife and son Nicholas, if afl ahve twelve pounds for mourning. Mary Parker and Richard Cross eight pounds for mourning. Thomas Williamson my grandson and his wife eight pounds for mourning. If any dead the less for the survivors, and would have evry one buy mourning for themselves, giving them timely notice thereof. And the reason for declaring what everyone must be paid for mourning is because I have given them what I design to give them in my lifetime and would not have them to have any more, and if they are not content with that, they can't displease me, being dead.

Wills and Testaments

Originally a Will dealt with real estate and a Testament with personalty, but for a long time it has been the practice to combine the two in one document. In this Short Guide the word Will is used to cover both.

The Probate Division of the High Court of Justice, together with the District Probate Courts or Registries commenced to function — under the Probate Act Of 1857 — on 12 January 1858. Before that date probate was, in the main, granted by a great variety of ecclesiastical and secular courts, although of these there were three principal types. Normally it was to the court of the bishop of the diocese in which the deceased's property lay that the executors applied, but if such property were in more than one diocese the appropriate authority was the prerogative court of the archdiocese.

For smaller estates probate could be granted by archdeacons and rural deans. Several lay courts had probate jurisdiction, such as the Court of Hustings in London, the chancellors of Oxford and Cambridge universities and boroughs such as Lincoln. In addition were many Testamentary Peculiars which were generally manors belonging to both laymen and clerics, or sometimes were ecclesiastical parishes.

Though the Short Guide is concerned with Wills it may be useful to refer briefly to some other types of documents which may be found among official Probate Records. Most valuable are, of course, the inventories. Then there are Administration Bonds (Admons.) entered into by administrators of the estate of an intestate. They are very formal documents but have a value to the genealogist as the person appointed was normally a close relative. The genealogist also benefits from the Tuition or Curation Bond, which provides for the guardianship of minors or incompetent persons. Occasionally the will is accompanied by a set of executors' accounts. If any dispute arose from the execution of a will or administration the matter went before an ecclesiastical court, as a result of which it sometimes happens that the interrogatories and depositions are attached to the original will or administration bond.

The Act Books record when and to whom probate or administration was granted and in many courts wills have been enrolled, that is, full copies have been entered into registers.

Format

Wills are normally written on paper or parchment, but may vary in size from a single small to twenty or more large sheets. Only in very early ones is the language other than English, but the text, even in comparatively modern wills, may be of a very informal nature. Up to the middle of the eighteenth century it was the custom for the opening phrases to be of a religious nature, bequeathing at great length the soul to God and the body to Christian burial in a specified place.

Gradually, as testamentary law grew in complication, formality of phrase developed and the amount of legal jargon grew to such an extent that for information which could be written by the historian in ten words the lawyer used a hundred, or even more. Administration and tuition bonds are normally on a single sheet of foolscap paper, the large formal portion of which is printed. Act books and registers may be of either paper or parchment and vary much in size, some being very thick and unwieldy.

Location

For wills after 1857 there are only two places to enquire — the District Probate Registaries and the Principal Probate Registry in Somerset House, The Strand, London. In this latter repository are also the pre-1858 wills proved in the Prerogative Court of Canterbury. Very many of the pre-1858 wills of all the other courts are now in the various county record offices and enquiries should always be made to the appropriate one of these. The tremendous multiplicity of courts which, before 1858, had testamentary jurisdiction is such that it is absolutely essential for a searcher to consult the invaluable *Wills and Their Whereabouts* in its edition of 1963 by A.J. Camp and published by the Society of Genealogists.

Another source of wills is the muniments of private families, which, when no longer in the custody of the family, will usually be found in the local record office, borough or county, or possibly in the local library. Most of the wills in family collections are what are called probate-copies which are in effect copies of the will (the original being retained in the probate court) accompanied by the official act of probate which allowed the executors to proceed with their duties. Sometimes, especially in earlier times, the court returned the original will to the executors and kept a copy among its own records. There may also be found in the private muniments wills which for one reason or another were never proved, or undestroyed wills which were superseded by later ones. It was not uncommon prior to the middle of the eighteenth century for there to be no probate where estates were small or disputes unlikely.

Uses

Let it be stated at once that the contents of wills vary greatly in their value to the historian; some are very disappointing in the detail they give, while others are veritable gold-mines of information. Though very much a generalisation, the later ones are often less rewarding than the earlier. There is no doubt that the greatest value of probate records is the information which they contain about family relationships; sometimes, in addition to bequests to relatives, quoting family and marriage settlements. They can also, especially when written without the aid of a lawyer, cast light upon the personality of the testator and help to 'bring him to life' as it were.

Research other than genealogical can, however, be forwarded by consulting probate records. Not only inventories but the wills themselves can cast light upon social, domestic and trade conditions by means of individual bequests of furniture, clothing and other goods. Charities were more frequently created by will than in the lifetime of the creator and although the majority of charities were for the benefit of the poor one finds many references to schools, churches and other institutions; also, especially in earlier wills, made in the days before the creation of 'local authorities', contributions were made to the upkeep of roads and bridges. Indications of local dialect and pronunciation are often to be found as phonetic spelling was not uncommon in the days before dictionaries and gazetteers. A warning against too literal an acceptance of relationships as stated in wills might perhaps be given: cousin indicated almost any degree of relationship; sons and daughters, mothers and fathers, brothers and sisters were often so called in instances in which we would today add the words 'in-law'; and grandchildren were sometimes called nephews and nieces. The term 'natural' son or daughter only at a later period might indicate illegitimacy — a condition which was usually quite openly stated. The word 'clerk' usually, before the nineteenth century, indicated a clergyman, while the descriptions 'husbandman' and 'yeoman' were usually an indication of social status rather than of occupation or even of substance.

Bibliography

Camp, Anthony J, *Wills and Their Whereabouts* (1963)
Gardener, D E and **Smith, F**, *Genealogical Research in England & Wales* (Vol. 2, pp. 53-143, 1952)
Jones, B C, 'The Lancashire Probate Records', *Trans. Hist. Soc. of Lancs. & Ches.* vol 104 (1952)
Loveless, Peter, *The Disposal of a Person's Estate by Will and Testament* (1792).
Swinburne, H, *A Briefe Treatise of Testaments and Last Willes* (1611).

Indexes of many groups or probate records have been published by the Index Library and local societies. The following are mere examples:
Archdeaconry of Cornwall, 1569-1800 (Index Library)
Consistory of Gloucester, 1541-1800 (Index Library)
Consistory of Chester and Rural Deancries, 1545-1825 (Rec. Soc. Lancs. & Ches.)
Archdeaconry of Richmond (Lancashire Deaneries), 1457-1858 (Rec. Soc. Lancs. & Ches.)
Prerogative Court of Canterbury, 1383-1700 (Index Library, except 1630-1652)
London Court of Hostings, 1258-1688
Consistory of Norwich, 1370-1686 (Norfolk Record Society)
Prerogative Court of York, 1389-1688 (Yorkshire Archaeological Society)

Recusant Rolls

J Anthony Williams

[P.R.O. Series E 377/76, Wiltshire portion of 1681 Roll illustrating (a) lands and tenements forfeited for recusancy and (b) the lunar-monthly fine of twenty pounds. The entries are printed below: (i) in transcript, showing the customary abbreviations, and (ii) in translation.]

a. i. Tenen' duar' pare' Terr' & Tentor' Eliz Trime vid' deb' xls. per Ann' de ffirm' duar' parc' un' tent' in Sutton mandevile & x acr' terr' Arr' duar' acr' past' & di'acr'prat'ibm Ann' Val 'lxs. De Terr' & Tentis pd Eliz Trime vid' Recusan' In man' Dni Rs nuc seit' ut supra Sicut contur ibm ET xls. de Arr' ET xls. pro vic' de Anno preden' Sicut contur in compo suo in Ro preden' in Wiltes pro Recusan' Sma vi 1. De quib' Vic' r' xls. in Dorso Rotli ET deb' iiii 1.

b. i. Wilhnus Hodges de Russell yeom' xx l pro cons' ibm. Anna uxor eius xx l pro cons' ibm. Jacobus Harward de Wamberough yeom' xx l pro cons' ibm.

a. ii. The tenants of two parts of the lands and tenements of Elizabeth Trime widow owe 40s. per annum for the farm of two parts of a tenement in Sutton Mandeville and ten acres of arable land, two acres of pasture and half an acre of meadow there, of the annual value of 60s.; Of the lands and tenements of the aforesaid Elizabeth Trime widow, Recusant, now seized into the hands of the Lord King as is contained above; And 40s. of arrears; and 40s. for the Sheriff of the preceding year as is contained in his account in the preceding Recusant Roll under Wiltshire. Total £6, for 40s. of which the Sheriff answers on the back of the Roll. And they [the tenants] owe £4.

b. ii. William Hodges of Rushall, yeoman, £20 for the like (i.e. for absence from his parish church).
Ann(a), his wife, £20 for the like.
James Harward of Wansborough, yeoman, £20 for the like.

Location

The Recusant Rolls of the Exchequer are annual rolls of sheriffs' accounts relating to recusants' fines and forfeitures and are preserved at the Public Record Office (series E. 377/1-82). They span exactly one hundred years, from 1592 to 1691, inclusive, but there are less than a hundred rolls because some contain entries for more than one year and some years are missing altogether; it is not until 1673 that an unbroken series for Charles II's reign begins. For the preceding thirteen years there are only three incomplete rolls together with some fragments in a bundle, marked 'Various Dates', composed mainly of early seventeenth-century rotulets (no. 82 of the series, the final roll in chronological order being no. 81). However, entries from Recusant rolls now missing, as well as from the Charles II portions of roll no. 82, were copied in 1671 into a large manuscript volume (British Museum, Add. MS. 20739) and printed in 1901 — not very accurately — in volume 6 of the Catholic Record Society's publications. The first Recusant Roll was printed in C.R.S. vol. 18 and the second appears in vol. 57, with a detailed introduction by Dom Hugh Bowler OSB.

Origin

Recusants were those who absented themselves from the services of the Established Church and so became liable, under the Act of Uniformity of 1559 (1 Eliz. I, cap. 2), to a fine of twelve pence for each absence, to be collected by the churchwardens for the relief of the poor of the parish; but in 1581 (23 Eliz. I, cap. 1) recusancy became an Exchequer matter with the introduction of a penalty of twenty pounds per lunar month. Later Acts (28 & 29 Eliz. I, cap. 6; 3 & 4 Jac. I, cap. 4) empowered the Crown to seize all a recusant's goods and two-thirds of his lands and tenements in lieu of the monetary fine. From 1581 to 1591 the penalties due from convicted recusants were entered on the Pipe Rolls but in 1592 a separate series was begun, devoted entirely to recusancy, and it is in these Rolls that recusants' fines and forfeitures, as returned by the sheriff, are recorded for the next hundred years.

Format

Each Recusant Roll comprises a series of parchment rotulets arranged in roughly alphabetical order under English counties (though Yorkshire, of course, occurs as Ebor, Hampshire as Southampton and Worcestershire as Wigorn) followed by the whole of Wales (Wallia). Durham entries occur in the Ebor section and London and Middlesex may be combined, as may Surrey and Sussex. Occasionally rotulets may be misplaced or may lack a county-heading, while a rotulet headed with the name of one county may have entries for another added after its own, late-coming items being added in any vacant space in the Roll. Occasionally there are 'clerical errors' in the Rolls themselves, e.g. in Roll E. 377/68 two dozen recusants are listed for the Wiltshire parish of Stoke Forthing ('Stoake Verdon'), the first having the parish noted after his name and status and the others being marked *de eadem*. However, the original presentment shows that only the first three were of that parish; the remaining twenty-one were of the strongly Catholic parish of Stourton (now Stourhead). This underlines the importance of checking the Rolls themselves against other documents wherever possible. But in view of the vast number of entries the standard of accuracy appears to be reassuringly high and the documents can be used with some degree of confidence.

All entries are in Latin and embody numerous conventional abbreviations. The layout of the rotulets is consistent throughout the century of their existence; after a preamble giving the name and other particulars of the county's sheriff responsible for making the returns embodied in it, each begins with entries relating to the forfeited two-thirds seized by the Crown (see example a) and concludes with estreats of conviction for recusancy (example b) relating to the lunar-monthly fine of twenty pounds. Each rotulet normally contains these two types of entry, but others may sometimes occur between them; e.g. statements of sheriffs' arrears and entries relating to goods and chattels which have been seized in accordance with the Statutes mentioned above. Very occasionally, too, other penalties may be encountered: fines for hearing Mass or for defiance of the Ecclesiastical Commission. The bulk of the entries, however, are those relating to the two-thirds forfeitures and to the twenty-pound fine. There is little variation in the wording of the latter; they merely repeat that the named recusant owes £20 or a multiple of it for 'the same reason' (i.e. for persistent absence from his parish church), but there is less uniformity about the first type of entry, relating to the disposal of the forfeited two-thirds. As can be seen (from example a) the entry gives the name and status of the convicted recusant, particulars of the lands seized and leased by the Crown and the sums owing in respect of rental and arrears. Other information may be given; e.g. fuller particulars of the seizure, including the name of the commissioner responsible for it, details of buildings and goods and even of horses, stock, etc., and perhaps the note '*ET QUIETUS EST*' indicating that the liability had been discharged, either by payment or, as in the case of William Moore of Chilmark, Wilts. (P.R.O. E. 377/78), by conformity. Receipts (or quietuses) given to the payers of recusancy fines are to be found among Catholic family papers, such as those of the Eystons and the Throckmortons (see, respectively, *Hist. Mss. Commission, 3rd Report, Appendix*, p. 261, and *10th Report, Appendix IV*, p. 17 1; also B. Camm, *Forgotten Shrines* (1910), 397-8 — Quietus granted to Anthony Fitzherbert of Padley, Derbyshire, 1606).

The Uses of Recusant Rolls

It would be a mistake to suppose that a study of the Recusant Rolls will necessarily reveal the names of most of the recusants, or the distribution of recusancy, in a county. Nor do they reveal the extent to which fines were actually imposed upon convicted recusants; they are records of indebtedness, not of payment. Under Elizabeth I the highest number of recusants paying the full penalty in any one year was seventeen; little over £6000 was received in the year 1594-5; the Budget for 1600 puts the revenue from recusancy at not much more than £700 and the total receipts from this source for the five years from Easter 1680 to Easter 1685 amounted only to some £12,000 (P.R.O., Pells Receipt Books, E. 40 1 /1965-1975). During the first decade of Charles 11's reign very few recusancy fines were collected and the nobility and 'considerable gentry' make little appearance in the 1671 return.

However, the disparity between sums due and sums levied is itself worthy of investigation and it is only from the Recusant Rolls that we can discover the former. The constant recurrence of the £20 fine is an indication of persistent recusancy — often discoverable only from the Recusant Rolls — and the data given in the other types of entry have an obvious value to the social and economic historian. For names and relationships, status and location the Recusant Rolls are of interest to the genealogist as well as to the ecclesiastical historian, while the detailed particulars of lands, fields, forests, etc. (sometimes even to the name of a house or farm) provide a rich quarry for the student of place- names. The Recusant Rolls are important also because their bulk, or lack of it, may be an index to the intensity of official action against Catholics and separatists, while the non-conviction of notorious and well-to-do recusants, indicated by the absence of their names from the Recusant Rolls, is another matter calling for investigation.

By no means all of those listed in the Recusant Rolls are *popish* recusants as has too often been supposed. Even in Elizabeth's reign the rolls include the names of protestant sectaries; e.g. a Brownist and his wife in Bath (see my *Bath and Rome, the Living Link*, Bath, 1963, p. 8) and in the later Rolls large numbers of dissenters — often outnumbering Romanists — are included. The Rolls themselves seldom indicate a recusant's religious allegiance, but this can often be ascertained from the initial presentment of the offender, either at an ecclesiastical Visitation or at Quarter Sessions. An investigation of all the Wiltshire presentments, both ecclesiastical and civil, between 1663 and 1691 has revealed the presence in the Recusant Rolls of dissenters of all kinds ('Anabaptists', Quakers, some Fifth Monarchists and even a 'reputed Jew') and suggests that these documents may be as important a source of Nonconformist as of Roman Catholic history.

Bibliography

Bowler, Dom Hugh OSB, *Introduction to Catholic Record Society* (vol. 57) also 'Some Notes on the Recusant Rolls of the Exchequer', *Recusant History*, Vol. 4, no.5 (Bognor Regis, 1958), pp. 182-98, and 'Corrigenda and Addenda' in *Recusant History*, vol. 4, no. 6, p. 243

Havran, M J, *The Catholics in Caroline England* (1962)

Magee, B, *The English Recusants* (1938)

Wigfield, W M, 'Religious Statistics Concerning Recusants of the Stuart Period', *Theology* XLI (August l940), pp.94 *et seq*

Williams, J. Anthony, 'Some Sidelights on Recusancy Finance Under Charles II', *Dublin Review* (Autumn 1959), pp.245-53

Williams, J Anthony, 'Recusancy and Dissent in Wiltshire, 1663-1691: The Evidence of the Recusant Rolls', in *A Newsletter for Students of Recusant History*, no.4 (compiled by Professor T. A. Birrell, Van Nispenstraat 19, Nijmegen, the Netherlands), pp. 21-2. [Synopsis of a paper read at the fourth Oxford Conference on Post-Reformation Catholic History, April 1961]

Deeds of Title

A D Carr

The Feoffment

[Buckinghamshire Record Office A.R.33/61]
This Indenture ... made the eighth day of February ... 1663 [1664] between Sir John Packington of Westwoods in the county of Worcester, baronet, and Dame Dorothy, his wife, of the first part, Anthony Lord Ashley [and four others] of the second part and William Dawney of Aylesbury in the county of Bucks., innholder, of the third part ... witnesseth that they, the said Anthony Lord Ashley [etc.] by the limitation and appointment of the said Sir John Packington ... have granted, aliened, bargained, sold, enfeoffed and confirmed and by these presents do grant, alien, bargain, sell, enfeoff and confirm unto the said William Dawney, his heirs and assigns, for ever, all that messuage or tenement with the appurtenances commonly ... called King's Head Inn with two pieces of waste ground thereunto adjoining ... in Aylesbury aforesaid ...
The *Endorsement* records that on 29 September, 1664 'full and peaceable possession and seisin' of the property was given by the attorney of Ashley (then Chancellor of the Exchequer) and his fellows to Dawney in the presence of witnesses whose signatures are appended.

The Feoffment was the most ancient form of conveyance. It was not the actual written deed which conveyed the land; it was the *livery of seisin*, the physical entry into the property in the presence of witnesses. The significant part of the deed was the endorsement, which recorded the entry; without it enfeoffment had not taken place and the document was meaningless. Feudal law insisted on the public transfer of land in order to prevent a tenant escaping from any duties or conditions. The subsequent history of conveyancing is the history of the various measures devised by lawyers to evade this requirement and convey land without the public ceremony. A relic of livery of seisin survived in the phrasing of certain deeds. The dispositive clause ('have granted ...') appeared first of all in the past tense, as if livery had already taken place; it was then repeated in the present tense.

The Bargain and Sale

[Gloucestershire Record Office, G G 688]
This Indenture made the five and twentieth day of November in the one and twentieth year of the reign of our sovereign lord James ... Between John Winchcombe of Henwick in the county of Berks., esq, and Joseph Baynham of Westbury in the county of Gloucester, gent, of the one part, and John Cotton of Suberton in the county of Southampton, esq, of the other part Witnesseth that ... the said John Winchcombe and Joseph Baynham for and in consideration of the sum of one hundred pounds ... well and truly paid by the said John Cotton ... have ... granted, bargained, sold, aliened and confirmed and by these presents do fully and absolutely grant ... unto the said John Cotton ... All the said cottage or tenement, iron mill and three acres of land ... together also with all and all manner of implements, instruments, tools, utensils, wheels, hammers, anvils and other necessaries and other things...

Short Guides to Records 12

Deeds of Title

Medieval lawyers devised the *Use*, by which the vendor could transfer property to a nominal purchaser to hold to the use of or for the benefit of a third party; thus the second party was the legal owner but the effective owner was the third party, who escaped feudal duties and restrictions. To combat this the Statute of Uses was passed in 1536; henceforth, when a use was *raised*, the estate passed at once to the third party, despite the conveyance to his trustee, and he alone was recognized as proprietor. In reply the lawyers evolved the *Bargain and Sale*. The vendor 'bargained and sold' the property to the purchaser and was then deemed to hold it temporarily to his use. Under the Statute this meant that the land passed at once to the purchaser as the use created was immediately *executed* in his favour. Thus the whole transaction was speedily and secretly completed by the very statute aimed to overcome secret conveyances. The Statute of Enrolments of 1536 recognized the practice but sought to defeat the secrecy by stipulating that Bargains and Sales must be *enrolled in a court* within six months; many of these deeds will therefore be found to bear a record of this enrolment in a formal handwriting.

The Lease and Release

[Essex Record Office, D/DEt T7]

(i) The Lease. This Indenture made the twenty sixth day of January ... in the year of our Lord one thousand seven hundred and fifty nine Between Eli Jackson of Aldham in the county of Essex, tailor, of the one part, and Bezaleel Angier of Colchester in the said county, maltster, of the other part Witnesseth that for and in consideration of the sum of five shillings ... to him in hand paid by the said Bezaleel Angier ... he, the said Eli Jackson, hath bargained and sold ... unto the said Bezaleel Angier ... All that messuage or tenement ... AND ALSO ALL THAT windmill erected upon parcel of the land called Gogglefield, together with the hill whereon the said windmill stands, with the boulting, mill wheels, sails, stones, brasts and ironwork ... situate ... in the parish of Saint James and Saint Nicholas or one of them in Colchester ... to have and to hold the said messuage or tenement, windmill ... unto the said Bazaleel Angier ... for, during and unto the term of one whole year ... yielding and paying therefore unto the said Eli Jackson ... the rent of one pepper corn only on Michaelmas day next ensuing ... to the intent that by virtue of these presents and by force of the Statute for transferring uses into possession, he, the said Bezaleel Angier, may be in the actual possession of all and singular the said messuage [etc] ... and thereby enabled to accept and take a grant and release of the reversion and inheritance thereof ...

(ii) The Release. This Indenture made the twenty seventh day of January ... [parties as in the Lease of the previous day] ... Witnesseth that for and in consideration of two hundred pounds ... hath granted, bargained, sold, aliened, released and confirmed and by these presents doth grant ... unto the said Bezaleel Angier (in his actual possession now being by virtue of a Bargain and Sale to him thereof made for one whole year by the said Eli Jackson by indenture bearing date the day next before the day of the date hereof and by force of the Statute for transferring Uses into possession) ... All that [properties as in Lease] ... and the reversion and reversions, remainder and remainders, rents, issues and profits ... To have and to hold for ever ...

This was the most effective and popular of the forms of conveyance spawned by the Statute of Uses; it not only escaped the many existing restrictions on the free disposal of land but was also devised in such a way as to preclude subsequent inhibition. In form it was delightfully simple; the vendor first leased the land for six months or a year at a token rent, *bargaining and selling* it to the purchaser. The lease brought the purchaser into actual possession. On the following day the vendor conveyed the *reversion* of the lease to the purchaser; this was all that remained to him, and as it was not the land itself but only a right, called by the lawyers an *incorporeal hereditament*, it could be transferred without livery of seisin. And, as the lease was not freehold, there was no need for enrolment in the courts. It remained the most widespread form of conveyance until the repeal of the Statute of Uses in 1845 and is the easiest of all deeds to recognize, consisting as it does of two documents bearing consecutive dates, the smaller often being tucked inside the other.

The Final Concord

[Essex Record Office, D/DGe 641]
This is the final agreement made in the Court of our Sovereign Lord the King at Westminster on the Monday of All Souls in the thirtieth year of the reign of George the Third ... before Justices of our Lord the King, others then there present. Between Thomas Frost Gepp, plaintiff, and John Wallinger Arnold, esq., deforciant, of one messuage, two barns, four stables, six curtilages, two gardens, twelve acres of land, six acres of meadow, six acres of pasture ... in the parish of Chelmsford. Whereupon a plea of Covenant was summoned between them in the same court, that is to say that the aforesaid John Wallinger Arnold, hath acknowledged the aforesaid tenements ... to be the right of him, the said Thomas Frost as those which the said Thomas Frost hath of the gift of the aforesaid John Wallinger Arnold and these he hath Remised, Quitclaimed from him and his heirs to the afore said Thomas Frost.

Certain fictitious legal actions were devised to facilitate the transfer of land. The Fine, quoted above, took the form of proceedings begun by the purchaser, *plaintiff*, against the vendor, *deforciant*, alleging that he had, at some previous date, unjustly deprived him of the land in question. The parties went to court but, before judgement was given, they reached a compromise under which the plaintiff was to have the land and the deforciant a sum of money which was, in actual fact, the purchase price. The action took place in the Court of Common Pleas and was recorded on the rolls of that tribunal. The deed took the form of a copy of the enrolment made in triplicate on a single sheet of parchment, a *tripartite indenture*. Copies were given to each of the parties and the third copy, the *Foot of the Fine*, remained with the court. The Feet of Fines are preserved in the Public Record Office; the Final Concords preserved in private archives are those given to the litigants. The action was preceded by a deed known as the *Covenant to Levy a Fine*, but neither this nor the Final Concord contain any topographical information more detailed than that quoted above. According to the twelfth-century jurist, Glanville, the deed was called a Final Concord because it put an end to the transaction.

The Common Recovery

[UCNW, Bangor, Kinmel MS. 343]

[1735] ... Denbigh. John Pulford, gent., in his own person ... doth demand against John Lloyd, gent., 5 messuages, 2 cottages, l5 acres of land [etc.] ... with the appurtenances in Bodtegwall, Towyn, Bodorryn, Abergeley and Gwrych in the parish of Abergeley ... as his right and inheritance and into which the aforesaid John Lloyd hath not entry unless after the disseizin which Hugh Hunt thereof unjustly and without judgement made to the aforesaid John Pulford within thirty years ... And the aforesaid John Lloyd in his own person doth come and defend his right etc. and thereupon doth call to warranty David Hughes and William Hughes who are present here in court in their own persons and freely do warrant to him the tenements aforesaid ... and hereupon the aforesaid John Pulford doth demand against the aforesaid David and William tenants by their warranty, the tenements aforesaid ... And the aforesaid David and William, tenants by their warranty, do defend their right ... and thereupon do further call to warranty James Roxbrugh ... and the aforesaid James, tenant by his warranty, doth defend his right ... and saith that the aforesaid Hugh Hunt did not disseize the aforesaid John Pulford of the tenements aforesaid ... and the aforesaid John Pulford doth desire liberty thereupon to imparle and he hath it etc. and afterwards the aforesaid John Pulford came again here into court ... in his own person and the aforesaid James, although solemnly called, came not but went away in contempt of the court and made default. Therefore it is considered that the aforesaid John Pulford do recover his seisin against the aforesaid John Lloyd of the tenements aforesaid ... and that the said John Lloyd have of the lands of the aforesaid David and William to the value etc. and that the same David and William further have of the lands of the aforesaid James to the value etc. and the same James in mercy etc. ...

Another fictitious action was the Common Recovery. In this the *recoverer* (i.e. the purchaser) sued the *tenant* (i.e. the vendor) from whom the land was to be acquired, alleging that he had no legal title, having come into possession after a supposed Hugh Hunt (a stock fictitious name) had turned the recoveror out. The tenant appeared and defended his right, *vouching to warranty* a third party, the *vouchee*, who, at the original purchase, was supposed to have assured the tenant of the title and who therefore was bound to replace him in defending it. Formally, the recoveror then sought leave of the court to *imparl* — that is, to confer with the vouchee; when the court reassembled the vouchee of course failed to appear and judgement was given for the recoveror. The tenant was to have land of equal value from the vouchee who had, in theory, misled him as to the title, but the vouchee had no land, being usually the court cryer. The land in dispute was consequently absolutely vested in the recoveror by judgement of the court, so the action operated as a conveyance. As a rule, however, the first vouchee would vouch a fourth party to warranty as in the case quoted above; this form was known as recovery by *double voucher*, the simpler form being by *single voucher*. After Tudor times recoveries were almost invariably by double or even treble voucher. In England the action was carried out in the Court of Common Pleas and in Wales at the Great Sessions; it could also be heard in a manorial court. The transaction was entered on the rolls of the court and the deed, a copy of the entry, is described as an *exemplification* of the action, an ornate document bearing the royal portrait. The topographical information is as nebulous as that contained in the Final

Concord and like the Fine the action was preceded by a deed — the *Deed to Lead the Uses of a Recovery*. Both Fine and Recovery, being copies of entries on the rolls of the courts, were in Latin until 1733, though in English during the Commonwealth.

Format

Deeds of title come in all shapes and sizes, ranging from the medieval grant a few inches long to the eighteenth-century Lease and Release of a large estate, naming not only all the farms but their component fields and running to ten or a dozen skins of parchment, each a yard square. Apart from the Final Concord and the Common Recovery, which have already been discussed, they were generally written in Latin until about the middle of the sixteenth century, when English became almost universal. There are, of course, exceptions either way. Many deeds bear seals, ranging from the elaborate medieval armorial examples to the eighteenth-century (and later) gummed wafer which was appended beside each signature; a Common Recovery 'suffered' (the technical term) in the Court of Common Pleas bears the pendent seal of the court, often encased in a tin box or skippet. If a deed has neither seal nor signature it has very probably not been executed; the transaction it records was never completed. If it has a herring-bone pattern of cuts across it, it means that it has been cancelled; the operation was carried out by folding the document once and cutting several times.

The Uses of Deeds of Title

The Law of Property Act of 1925 which limited the need for evidence of title to thirty years meant that the retention of earlier deeds was no longer necessary. Consequently there has since been a steady flow, even a torrent of them, into record repositories. They can be put to a variety of uses. The preambles often contain valuable information for the genealogist but their value to the student lies above all in the mass of detailed topographical information which they contain. The urban historian, attempting to reconstruct the layout of an eighteenth-century street or to trace the extent of Victorian building development, is dependent on them. The information they contain is invaluable to the historical geographer or to the economic historian interested in the growth and management of a large estate; the process of growth, in particular, can be traced by means of the title deeds. They are, too, extremely useful to the amateur historian interested in his own house or locality. The information furnished by deeds of title can include the names of properties, their location in relation to their neighbours, field-names, acreages, cultivation, occasionally small but detailed maps and sometimes, in the case of houses, inventories of fixtures and furnishings.

Bibliography

Blackstone, *Commentaries on the Laws of England* (15th edn. ed. Christian, E, London, 1809, II), pp 295-343

Cornwall, Julian, *How to Read Old Title Deeds* (University of Birmingham, Department of Extra-Mural Studies, 1963)

Digby, K E, *An Introduction to the History of the Law of Real Property* (4th edn. Oxford, Clarendon Press, 1892)

Foster, Amy, *Conveyancing Practice from Local Records*, reprinted from *Thoresby Miscellany*, vol 12, Part II, (Leeds, 1948)

Pugh, R B, *Calendar of Antrobus Deeds before 1625* (Devizes, Wilts. Archaeological Society, 1947) in introduction

Simpson, A W B, *An Introduction to the History of Land Law*, (OUP, 1961) chapters VI and VIII

Glebe Terriers

D M Barratt

[Extracts from a terrier of the rectory of Kencott, Oxon., of 1683 among the Oxford archdeaconry records in the Bodleian Library, Oxford, MS. Archd. papers Oxon. b. 41 f 9.)

A Terrier of all the Housing, Tithes and Glebe lands belonging to the Rectory of Kencot in the Diocesse of Oxon.

Imprimis A Dwelling House consisting of five Bay of building, a Brewhouse adjoyning of three Bay, a Carthouse and Woodhouse of three Bay, two Barnes each of foure Bay, a Sheepe house of sixe Bay, Gardens, Courts, Backside & Rickbartons being together about one Acre of Ground.

All manner of Tithes great & small except milke, in lieu of which each new milch Cow payes two pence and a thorow milch Cow three half pence.

....

Offrings of all persons above the age of sixteene yeares, being two pence payable at Easter yeerely.

One Close of Meadow Ground adjoyning to the Backside of the said Dwelling House conteyning about one Acre & an halfe.

....

One Acre of Meadow Ground lying in the Meadows belonging to Kencot commonly knowne by the name of the Thames Meadows.

One half Acre of Meadow Ground in a place called Astwell adjoyning to the Arrable Land & Shooting upon the Leaze hedge.

Commons for five Horses, ten Rother Beasts, six score Sheep, & one Bull.

Seventy eight Acres [1] of Arrable Land in both Fields as followeth:

Acres. [1]	halfe Acres. [1]	In the East Field
2	—	In the old Hitchin, one end abuting on the Towne, the other upon two headlands of Mr. Goddard Carter, on the North the hedge by the high way, on the South half an Acre of Thomas Hulet.
—	1	In Coppice end furlong, two half Acres of Adam Tumer South, & half an Acre of his North.
1	1	Lying crosse Burford way, one Acre of Adam Turner South, one & an half Acre of Will: Hulet North.

[In all 39 pieces totalling $41\frac{1}{4}$ 'acres' in East Field are similarly described, followed by 25 pieces totalling $36\frac{3}{4}1$ 'acres' in West Field.]

This is a true Terrier of what belongs to the Rectory of Kencot abovesaid taken the 22th day of September Anno Domini 1685 ... Testified by us [signatures or marks of the rector, two churchwardens and three other parishioners].

[1] *Acres and half acres in this sense are strips of certain widths, rather than a measurement of area.*

Description

Glebe terriers are surveys of the endowments of benefices compiled by incumbents and churchwardens, often with the help of their oldest or most substantial parishioners. As in this example, the largest part of a terrier usually consists of a description of the glebe land belonging to the living, but it will normally also be concerned with the parsonage house, tithes and offerings, and will describe any other less usual sources of income or privileges claimed by the incumbent. The bishop or archdeacon instructed the clergy and churchwardens to compile these surveys when he held a visitation, and they were directed to send them to the diocesan or archidiaconal registry to be preserved there as a permanent record. Their original purpose was to prevent encroachments on the glebe, but they were also often used as evidence in disputes about tithes and other dues.

The bishops were first directed to see that terriers of glebe land were compiled and deposited in their archives by a canon of 1571, and this instruction was repeated and enlarged in canon 87 of 1604. In most dioceses, therefore, the earliest surviving terriers belong either to the late sixteenth or to the early seventeenth century. The earliest now known are those of 1572 for Gloucester diocese. The frequency with which terriers were collected after 1604 varies in different areas, but every diocese appears to have at least some for the Stuart period. Later terriers where they exist are frequently copies of earlier ones.

In the large diocese of Lincoln an official, William Folkingham, was employed as 'general surveyor of church gleabes and possessions within the diocesse' in 1605-7, and all the Lincoln diocesan terriers of those years are made under Folkingham's supervision and set out in the same way. Normally, however, the compiling of the terriers was evidently left largely to the discretion of individual incumbents, and those collected at any one visitation often vary greatly in the amount of detail they give and in the form of arrangement they adopt. Usually the terriers were just bundled away when they reached the registries, but instances are known of registers of all the terriers sent in being compiled, and also of the originals being bound into a volume, two forms of protection against loss.

Location

As is obvious from the above, glebe terriers are found among diocesan and archidiaconal records. These may still be in the custody of registrars, but they are now more likely to have been deposited in a local record repository. A copy of the original terrier sent to the registry was often kept in the parish, either loose in the church chest or copied into a parish register. Terriers are therefore also found among parish records either in the incumbent's charge or deposited in a local record office.

The Uses of Glebe Terriers

The original purpose of glebe terriers was to describe the parish clergy's sources of income, and they therefore tell us much about the economic condition of the clergy, although they have as yet been less used for this subject than for others. They show whether an incumbent's income was in land, tithes and offerings, or was wholly or partly derived from a stipend. If, like the majority of clergy, he had land and tithes, the terriers always give an impression of how much land he had, and often state the quantity precisely. The terriers also show to which tithes of the parish the incumbent was entitled, and whether any of these tithes had been commuted for money or other forms of payment. With this information one can judge how the clergy would be affected by economic changes, and see why some livings got poorer while others became more valuable. Stipends and money payments in lieu of tithes declined in real value as prices rose, whereas a large glebe and the great tithes of corn and hay were endowments which tended to increase in real value. Terriers only occasionally give the value of the living, but where seventeenth or eighteenth century valuations are available from other sources, much can be learnt by comparing these figures with the 'king's book' values of livings (that is their values in the Valor Ecclesiasticus of 1535), and turning to terriers for explanations of exceptionally large or small increases in money value.

The detailed accounts of glebe land which many terriers contain are a valuable source both for agricultural history and for local topography and place names, especially in areas of open field cultivation. Similar terriers of private holdings were often compiled in this period, usually when a sale or lease of the holding was made, and some manorial surveys are also similar to glebe terriers in form. Sometimes the agricultural pattern of an individual parish can be reconstructed in detail from these other types of survey, and, especially if there is not much glebe, the ecclesiastical terriers will add little to the picture. Probably, however, no other single source in one repository throws as much light on the agricultural pattern of a whole district under the Stuarts as a diocesan collection of terriers.

Almost all terriers show whether the glebe is enclosed or lies mainly in open fields. Where there are open fields many throw light on how these are laid out (though only a few reveal what the rotation of crops was), and on the types of meadow and pasture found in the parish. The terriers also provide evidence about the progress of enclosures which is especially valuable in the seventeenth century when other sources are often lacking. Glebe may be in open fields in one terrier and enclosed in a later one, or there may just be incidental references to old or recent enclosures in descriptions of boundaries or of pasture rights. When an estate was enclosed or imparked the owner sometimes 'compounded' for his tithes, that is he arranged to make an annual payment or to give land to the incumbent in lieu of titles, and therefore enclosures and parks are also sometimes referred to when 'compositions' for tithes are described. H. L. Gray used the Oxfordshire glebe terriers in his study of English Field Systems as long ago as 1915, and Professor Beresford's more recent regional studies of open fields and enclosures are based almost entirely on terriers.

The approximate positions of the open fields of a parish and of the common meadows and waste grounds can often be deduced from detailed terriers like

Glebe Terriers

this of Kencott. Sometimes it is also possible to work out approximately where each furlong lay and in which direction the strips ran, especially if the student is prepared to explore the ground in person. The names of the furlongs often survive as names of modern fields, or if now forgotten can often be found on a tithe map. A mention of a road in the boundaries may be a valuable reference to a highway that has lost its former importance.

Some terriers contain descriptions of tithing customs of interest to both agricultural and social historians. Detailed lists of the titheable products of a parish, which are also sometimes found, may include an early reference to a new crop, or a useful mention of a special local product, such as woad, which is listed as titheable in a few Worcestershire terriers.

Finally, almost every benefice was endowed with a house for the incumbent and the descriptions of the parsonage house found in terriers are of interest to the student of domestic architecture. Terriers often give the size of both the house and the outbuildings in terms of 'bays' or 'spaces', and they occasionally list the rooms, mention recent additions or rebuilding, or specify building or roofing materials. The value of this information is very well illustrated by Mr. M. W. Barley's work, *The English Farmhouse and Cottage.*

Bibliography

Barrett, D M (ed), *Ecclesiastical terriers of Warwickshire parishes I, parishes, A — Li* (Dugdale Society, XXII, 1955) The introduction to this volume contains a fuller account of the history of this class of document, and an attempt to illustrate the uses of this particular collection.

Beresford, M W, 'Glebe terriers and open field Leicestershire' *Leics Archaeological Society Transactions,* XXIV, 1948 pp. 77-126

    'Glebe terriers and open field Yorkshire'; *Yorkshire Archaeological Journal,* XXXVIII, 1950 pp. 325-68

    'Glebe terriers and openfield Buckinghamshire' ; *Records of Bucks.,* XV, Pt. 5, 1951-2 pp. 283-98, XVI, Pt. 1, 1953-5, pp. 5-28

Ferguson, R S (ed), *Miscellany Accounts of the Diocese of Carlisle* (Cumberland and Westmorland Antiquarian and Archaeological Society, 1877), pp. 159-241.

Gloucester City Libraries *Local History Pamphlet* no. 4, (1964), is a handlist of the Gloucester diocesan terriers.

Enclosure Awards and Acts

W E Tate

TO ALL TO WHOM THESE PRESENTS SHALL COME we John Cleaver late of Castle Howard in the County of York but now of Carburton in the County of Nottingham Gentleman John Lund of Bootham in the Suburbs of the City of York Gentleman and John Owtram late of Burton Agnes otherwise Agnes Burton in the said County Gentleman send Greeting WHEREAS in and by an Act of Parliament passed in the ninth year of the Reign of his present Majesty George the third intituled AN ACT for dividing inclosing and draining certain open Fields Lands and Commons within the Townships of Sheriff Hutton and West Lilting in the Parish of Sheriff Hutton in the County of York WE the said [J.C., J.L. and J.O.] are appointed Commissioners for putting the said Act in Execution in such Manner and subject to such Rules Directions and Provisions as are therein prescribed and established concerning the same as in and by the said recited Act amongst divers other Things therein contained reference being had thereto will more fully and at large appear NOW THEREFORE ... [Leeds City Library Archives Department, DB/193].

Format and Location

After this preamble we come to the point. The Commissioners recount how they have taken their qualifying oaths and appointed a Surveyor and a Clerk and sworn them in. They tell how they have caused to be made 'a true and exact Survey and Admeasurement' of the lands concerned. They say how they have heard and adjudicated on all the claims submitted to them concerning these lands, and how they have drawn up their final 'Determination Judgment and Arbitration', signed, sealed and delivered (12 Jan. 1776). A copy of this they have enrolled (usually in one of the Courts at Westminster or with the Clerk of the Peace for the County but in this case in the statutory Registry of Deeds at Northallerton (2 Mar 1776); they have deposited the original in the parish chest of the place concerned; where it is, or should be, to this day.

This is a fairly typical enclosure award. The awards are almost invariably on parchment or vellum, as a rule with a large-scale plan of the place concerned after the Commissioners had done their work. Usually, and very inconveniently, the award is in roll form on anything from one or two up to fifty or sixty skins of parchment. Sometimes an award exists as a bound book, occasionally it is available only as an unofficial or semi-official paper copy in the local estate office, often now transferred to the County Record Office. There are, I estimate, rather more than 4,000 *Private* Enclosure Acts and Awards, with nearly 2,000 more awards made under the later Public *General* Acts 1836-45 and under private agreements. In all they must cover, in more or less detail, lands in perhaps half of the (10,000 odd) ancient parishes in England. The reader interested in inquiring whether there is or is not an enclosure award for his own parish may pursue his inquiries of the rector or vicar, or of the parish, urban district, borough or county borough council. It will probably save time if instead he inquires of the County Archivist in the County Record Office at the Shire or County Hall. Even if the C.R.O. does not hold the Enclosure Award, as an original or copy, the archivist is almost certain to know where it is.

The Uses of Enclosure Awards

The enclosure award, when there is one, is a major source of information on half a dozen or a dozen different aspects of the history of the place concerned. The primary purpose of the awards was at once to achieve and to register the change from the ancient methods of husbandry, the use of open field arable land, of common meadow and of common pasture — the common *par excellence* — to the modern system of land ownership, tenure and cultivation *in severalty*. But the awards have much more than merely legal or agro-technical interest and importance. They form the best — in many cases the only — source of accurate information as to the distribution of land ownership in English villages of a century and a half ago. They are full of useful information as to the types of land tenure prevalent in the different districts. In perhaps half the parishes of the country they serve as ultimate title deeds to a great part of the land, both that belonging to ordinary proprietors and that allotted to rectors, vicars, and lay impropriators in lieu of tithe and glebe.

They record the lands forming the endowments of ancient village charities and schools. They are the final authority for information as to the course and breadth of the highways, the existence of footpaths, bridle-ways, rights of way, and as to the courses and breadths, the liability for cleansing of most of the surface drains. The awards, and the plans generally appended to them register the ownership of hedges and other boundaries, as well as of the land's 'butts and bounds'. They may also distinguish among freeholds, leaseholds and copyholds of various classes, between titheable lands and those not liable to tithe. Many parishes in the Midlands had their tithes commuted largely under enclosure acts so that the enclosure awards in many counties are better sources of information as to the tithe than are the tithe awards. They specify the allotments of land for public purposes — generally to the parish surveyors of highways for use as parish gravel pits — which are the origins of the greater part of such land as still remains vested in the ownership of such minor local government bodies as parish councils and parish meetings. Accordingly the enclosure awards are invaluable sources of information to the historian or antiquary, whether his interest is mainly ecclesiastical or civil, economic or social.

Enclosure Acts

The awards do not, of course, tell the whole story. The historian studying the decisions set forth in his local enclosure award may well wish to turn backwards to the act under which it was made. Usually it is not difficult to do this. The enclosure acts are normally in the 'private' or 'local and personal' categories, which means that they are indexed in the *Statutes* but not printed there. Quite often when the award is a bound volume, a print of the act is bound in with it. Where it is in roll form sometimes the enrolled duplicate in the county records has a loose print of the act rolled up with it. Nearly all county record offices have a file of acts for their own areas, so have many leading local reference libraries, so, in many major provincial towns, have the district Law Societies.

The acts, especially those before 1801, contain a tremendous amount of common form, and the study of an individual act rarely yields a great deal to the inquirer, though the examination of say a dozen of the same date but for very different districts, or for neighbouring parishes but of a fairly wide date-range, may give interesting results.

The House of Commons Journal

If the student wants to go back further and discover what he can about the parliamentary proceedings on a particular act, he will find something, usually not much, about this in the printed *House of Commons Journal* (available to him by courtesy in the nearest university library). The *House of Commons Journal* for the reign of George III alone — the height of the period of parliamentary enclosure — occupies in print some forty-eight folio volumes (vols. 28-75). It is however very carefully indexed (it should be noted that the indexes are to the sessions, not to years or volumes, though there are some general index volumes, usually each covering about twenty years). Given the date, then, of one's own act, it is not hard to find the record of the proceedings on it. The student may care to note that the interesting details are nearly always found in the proceedings (a) on the presentation of the petition and the order that leave be given to prepare and bring in the bill, (b) on those of the Report Stage. All the other records are largely formal and rarely of any great interest.

Bibliography

In looking at any individual enclosure, the local historian will need to know what is the date of the act concerned, what is the area (if any) estimated in it, and which are the townships or parishes affected by it. Concerning the award, he will first try to find out where it is, or where an enrolled copy of it is to be seen, what was its date, and what acreage of open land was actually allotted by it — say some seven or eight items of legal, historical, chronological, statistical and archival information about each. These data cannot, unfortunately, be gathered from a single source. The following publications provide varying amounts of information.

The Annual Report of the Deputy Keeper of H.M. Public Records no. XXVII, 1866
Parliamentary Paper (House of Commons) no. 455, 1893
Parliamentary Paper (House of Commons) no. 50, 1904
Parliamentary Paper (House of Commons) no. 399, 1914
Slater, G, *The English Peasantry and the Enclosure of Common Fields* (1907)
The present author, **W E Tate**, has published *Handlists of Enclosure Awards* for many counties in the appropriate Society Transactions, and has in progress an index of all Parliamentary enclosures from 1603 to 1914. There is in the *Amateur Historian*, vol. 7, Spring 1963, a map of the country showing for which counties the handlists have already appeared in print.

Enclosure Awards and Acts

There are many general works on enclosure which the student may care to use in connection with his work on the awards. Of scholarly work on enclosure, its causes and its supposed consequences, perhaps the best, certainly the most readable, is **Hammond, J L and B**, *The Village Labourer*. If on studying this the inquirer feels, as probably he will, that he must sally out at once to shoot the squire, or at the least, spit on the grave of an enclosure commissioner, he had better first read **Curtler, W H**, *Inclosure and Redistribution of our Land*, a work of some literary merit (though of much less than the Hammonds' magnificent polemic) but one written from a quite opposite social and political viewpoint. The best recent treatment of the whole subject is **Parker, R A C**, *Enclosures in the Eighteenth Century*, in the Historical Association's 'Aids for Teachers' Series, No. 7 (1960) which contains also some useful critical bibliographical references

Chambers, J D and **Mingay, G E**, *The Agricultural Revolution 1750-1880* (London, 1966), is the most recent study of the background against which the enclosures took place.

Other Ancillary Sources of Information

If the inquirer wants to go back still further, and find out something about open-field agriculture in his parish long before enclosure, he should turn up for the earlier period any of the MS. sources exploited in Gray's *English Field Systems*. For eighteenth-century open-field agriculture in the county — if not the parish — the best source is the appropriate volume of the county reports / *General Views*, issued by the (first) Board of Agriculture from 1793 onwards. If the student is concerned rather with the social and economic results of enclosure, his best source is the Land Tax duplicates deposited among the county archives. These may be supplemented by the other Land Tax records, at this present moment being transferred to county record offices by the Commissioners of Inland Revenue upon the recent abolition of the Land Tax.

Records of Commissions of Sewers

A E B Owen

[Extracts from a book of sewers decrees and orders, 1660- 1706, among records of the Denge Marsh and Southbrooks Internal Drainage Board deposited in the Kent Archives Office, S/D SO 1.]

Dengmarish. A Generall Sessions of Sewers holden at Lydd in the County of Kent for the said Levell of Dengmarish on ... the sixt day of June ... 1682: Before Sir John Fagg Bart. [and 10 other Commissioners], and Godfrey Crosse Bayliffe of the said Levell..

.
At this present Sessions the Accompt of Thomas Godfrey Expenditour of this Levell of Dengmarish for the yeare past is fully examined and allowed by the Commissioners present according to the contents thereof entred in the Accompt Booke for that purpose ...
Whereas it doth appeare to the Commissioners here present by theire veiw and survay this day taken on the Sea Gutt at Dengnesse [i.e. Dungeness] in this Level that the same Gutt is wholly swerved and topped up with Beach and hath soe continued all the last Winter, and for that the said Gutt is very ruinous in the maine timbers and materialls thereof to the greate damage not only of the present occupiers of the lands in the said Levell but alsoe of the Owners of the Inheritance thereof ... And to the Intent the Commissioners ... may be fully satisfyed in the defect of the said Gutt and who or what lands ought to be charged with the repaires of the same, and may receive advantage or damage thereby, It is now ordered and decreed that severall precepts be forthwith directed to the Maiour of the Towne and Port of New Romney and the Bayliffe of the Towne of Lydd ... to returne a Jury of fower and twenty lawfull men in or neere the said Levell to enquire of the premisses and all other nusances ... in the said Levell and to appear at the George in Lydd to be impanelled ... [on 27 June] ...
At this present Sessions John Mascall gent. is elected and chosen Clerke of the said Levell of Dengmarish now void by the death of Mr. John Puckle ...

Commissions of Sewers

Commissioners of sewers dealt with the drainage of low-lying land and its protection against floods, whether of fresh or salt water. 'Sewer' here bears its original meaning of a watercourse, or channel for fresh water, and has nothing to do with the disposal of urban sewage. Although commissions in the London area had to devote much attention to the latter, theirs is a special case; in general, urban sanitation was no concern of commissioners of sewers. Commissions *de walliis et fossatis* (of walls and ditches) are first recorded in the later thirteenth century, but few records of medieval commissioners have survived and they need not be discussed here. A new era opened with the Statute of Sewers of l531 (23 Henry VIII c.5), on which subsequent drainage legislation was based. The Land Drainage Act of 1930 put an end to

Records of Commissions of Sewers

commissions of sewers (though some lingered on till after the Second World War), and their work is now done by internal drainage boards.

The courts of sewers, consisting of the commissioners meeting with a jury, had features in common with courts of quarter sessions, being like them both judical and administrative in character. Commissioners were drawn from the same class as justices of the peace and are sometimes called 'justices of sewers'. Commissions might be issued for part of a county, an area overlapping two counties (e.g. the Surrey and Kent Commission in what is now London south of the Thames), or an entire county. In the first two cases all the commissioners met customarily as a single court of sewers, but when one commission embraced a large county the practice was sometimes different; in Lincolnshire and Somerset local groups of commissioners constituted virtually autonomous courts, each administering a particular district of the county. Law and procedure, based ultimately on the ancient 'custom of Romney Marsh', were often much modified locally. The principal officer of each court was the clerk, who kept the records and was the linchpin of the organization. Other usual officers were an 'expenditor' or treasurer and a bailiff. In Lincolnshire and parts of adjacent counties the bailiff's place was taken by dikereeves, elected parish officers (usually two per parish) who were answerable to the court of sewers much as the constable was answerable to quarter sessions. A jury made presentments to the court as to the state of local drains and banks, and also 'presented' persons responsible for damage or neglect and those liable for repairs. In principle, those who benefited from works of drainage or sea defence ought to be assessed for their upkeep in proportion to the degree of benefit received. The rate (called in some places a 'scot') was usually based on acreage; distraint could be made for non-payment.

The earliest series of sewers records begin in the mid-sixteenth century. The main record of each court's business is a minute book, though in some parts of the country this appears under other names, e.g. 'order and decree book', 'court and order book' or 'presentment book', the term 'minute book' denoting only the draft of this record. The form of entry seems everywhere to be similar to the example from Denge Marsh here printed. Separate registers of orders and decrees only were often compiled. The many subsidiary classes of sewers records cannot be described here, but they often add much to the main record. In particular, from the late eighteenth century onwards such classes may prove more useful than the formal record of court sessions; for as the commissioners increasingly relied on reports of professional surveyors and engineers, the jurors' presentments diminished in value.

The statute of 23 Henry VIII was narrowly interpreted by the higher courts, who held that it conferred no power on commissioners of sewers to construct new works but only to maintain or improve existing ones. To overcome this difficulty, private Acts were obtained conferring on drainage commissioners or trustees the powers to execute works that might have been *ultra vires* for commissioners of sewers. As a result, much land was progressively withdrawn from the jurisdiction of sewers courts in favour of statutory commissions or trusts. These bodies lacked the judicial character of sewers courts, and their records, though equally interesting, are relatively conventional in form.

Uses of the Records

Records of commissioners of sewers are likely to be of interest for agricultural history. Though they may say little about crops, they can indicate the contribution of drainage rates to local farming costs, the seasonal employment provided by works of sewers, or the availability of pasture on coastal marshes. In East Lincolnshire routine maintenance work on drains and sea banks had a regular place in the farming year; as the demand for labour was often considerable, such works were usually carried out during May and early June in the slack period between seed-time and haymaking, continuing *diminuendo* until harvest, and resumed if necessary for a few weeks in October or November. There is also information on the use of the coastal sandhills for pasturage in this area. Indiscriminate grazing could destroy the vegetation which held these together, opening the way to sea floods. At Skegness in 1574 the commissioners prohibited grazing on the sea banks and adjacent marshes and appointed a pinder to enforce the order.

Since responsibility for maintaining drains and banks was often minutely subdivided, careful surveys had to be made for the sewers courts. These can give information on local patterns of landholding as well as topographical detail. One made of the Havering Levels in Essex in 1563 (it survives in a copy of *c.* 1720) records the lands in every marsh with their occupiers, indicates responsibility for works of sewers, and lists royal lands formerly monastic, showing the original monastic owner and present lessee. Fine examples of maps compiled for a similar purpose may be found in sewers records during the century before the Ordnance Survey established its monopoly of large-scale mapping. Earlier examples are worth looking for.

Records of those commissions responsible for sea defence works may be of value to historical geographers interested in coastal changes. At Dungeness (see above) the court of sewers had to act because the movement of shingle along the coast blocked the outfall of a land drain. In parts of Lincolnshire, where the sea has been encroaching since the thirteenth century, the sewers records tell in detail of sea banks repeatedly washed away and replaced. However, where the sea has receded and coastal marshes have been reclaimed, the records may prove disappointing, drainage of the reclaimed lands being often the responsibility of enclosure commissioners and not of the sewers courts.

There is often incidental information of interest. The earliest presentment book for the Havering Levels mentions water mills in south-west Essex, including paper mills in Walthamstow Level whose occupiers were ordered in 1697 not to pen the water at the mills higher than $4\frac{1}{2}$ feet. On the Lincolnshire coast much timber was needed for tidal sluicegates and breakwaters. The coastal marsh being largely treeless, supplies had to be brought from some distance (in 1579 timber for use at Ingoldmells came from Tattershall 25 miles away); the dikereeves' accounts sometimes give detailed particulars of such purchases, the cost of carpenters' supplies, and wages of seasonal labourers on the sea banks. The East Kent commissioners in 1684 ordered the dragging of an iron harrow at the stern of every lighter passing down the Stour from Fordwich to Sandwich — presumably a crude method of dredging. The commission's general expenditor was to provide 'three iron harrows of six foot in length with five beams and iron tines nine inches long with chains to drag them by'. Any lighterman negligent in this was to forfeit £3 6s. 8d. for each offence.

Location

On the dissolution of a commission of sewers following the Land Drainage Act of 1930, its records usually passed to its administrative successor, normally an internal drainage board or a river authority, but sometimes they remained with solicitors who were the last clerks to the commission. Many collections of sewers records are now in local record offices. Stray items sometimes appear among papers of families whose members served as commissioners, and in the Fens dikereeves' accounts and 'acre books' (surveys) may be in the parish chest.

Bibliography

Published *Guides* and *Reports* of local record offices (those of Essex, Kent, and Lincolnshire are particularly useful).

Court Minutes of the Surrey and Kent Sewer Commission, vol. 1 (covers the years 1569-79; no more published) (London County Council, 1909). These are the only published minutes of a commission of sewers.

Darlington, Ida, 'The London Commissioners of Sewers and their Records', *Journal of the Society of Archivists*, vol. ii, no. 5 (April 1962), pp. 196-210.

Cole, C N (ed), *Dugdale History of Imbanking and Draining*, 2nd edn., (London, 1772).

Kennedy, G G and **Sandars, J S**, *The Law of Land Drainage and Sewers* (London, 1884)

Kirkus, A Mary, *Records of the Commissioners of Sewers in the Parts of Holland, 1547-1603*, vol. 1. Lincoln Record Society, vol. 34 (1959). The introduction discusses the workings of commissions of sewers generally.

Owen, A E B, 'Land Drainage Authorities and their Records', *Journal of the Society of Archivists*, vol. ii, no. 9 (April 1964), pp 417-23

Webb, S and **B**, *English Local Government*, vol. IV (London, 1922), ch. 1, 'The Courts of Sewers'.

Land Tax Assessments

H G Hunt

An Assess made on the Parish of Ripple in the County of Kent the 30 April 1816. By virtue of An Act of Parliament for Grant His Majesty by A Land Tax of Four Shillings in the Pound

Landlords	Tenants	Rents		Exonerated	
Rev. Mr. Philpot	Himself	30	1 10		
Rob. Tolbart Esqr.	W. Garside	85	4 5		
Do.	M. Ralph	30	1 10		
J. B. Sladen Esqr.	Himself	96	4 16		
Wm. Thorn	Himself	86	4 6		
Joseph Marsh Senr.	R. Marsh	32	1 12		
Thomas Parker	Himself	2	2		
Stanley Parker	Himself	1	1		
Mr. Friend	Mrs. Nenstall	1	1		
Wm. Thorn	Himself	11		11	
Fleming Finch Esqr.	Himself	5		5	
John Brave Esqr.	Himself	16		16	
Geo. Leith Esqr.	G. Leith	15		15	
John Lade	Th. Cain	4		4	
Step. Carter	Himself	7		7	
Do.	Do.	2		2	
Do.	Geo. Newby	3		3	
Thos. Woodruff	W. Perkins	2		2	
J. B. Sladen, Esq.	Himself	4		4	
		£432	£18 3	£3 9	

The Land Tax Assessments are one of the chief documentary sources from which historians can trace changes in the ownership and occupation of the land in the period 1780-1832. The land tax was first established in 1692, but it is not possible to make systematic use of the returns until 1780 because of the defective way in which the early assessments were compiled, and because so few survive. From 1780 duplicate returns had to be lodged with the Clerk of the Peace to be used to establish voters' qualifications, and although this ceased to be necessary after 1832, the series, so produced, remains.

After 1780 most of the returns, which were drawn up annually, sometimes quarterly, list the names but not the profession or residence of owners of land in the parish, the names of occupiers (who, in most cases, were tenant farmers), and the sums which were payable. A good example of these assessments, that for the Parish of Ripple in Kent for the year 1816, is shown above.

Short Guides to Records 16

Land Tax Assessments

By comparing the names of the owners and occupiers and the sum of money for which their holdings were assessed, it is possible to make a study of the degree of consolidation of holdings, the size of farms and the incidence of absentee ownership in this critical period of English agrarian history. In the case of Ripple, Robert Tolbart Esqr. was the largest landowner in the parish, and his estate was divided into two large farms. William Thorn, who farmed his own land, was probably an example of the renowned Kentish yeomanry. The assessments of four shillings and under were most likely for buildings and adjacent land.

Location

The Land Tax Assessments from 1780-1832 constitute one of the best preserved series of records of the period. Most of the surviving assessments are to be found in the county record offices among the records deposited with the clerk of the peace and are usually arranged in parish bundles in chronological order. Since the assessments were originally drawn up in duplicate, it is not uncommon to find two copies of an assessment in the hands of the county archivist. Occasionally, copies are held in private collections, or in the parish chest, but rarely, if ever, do these sources contain long runs of assessments which can be used for studying changes over a period of time. Even in the county archives not all the parishes of the county are represented amongst the collection of assessments. Those for some parishes do not appear to have survived.

The Use of the Land Tax Assessments

A serious difficulty in the use of these records for historical research arises from the inconsistent way in which some of them were drawn up. Proprietors were normally, but not invariably, listed in the left-hand column, and the occupiers in the right-hand column. But because names were well-known locally and because the occupiers often actually paid the money, clerks occasionally failed to put a heading to the lists of names and reversed the order of the two columns. In cases where no heading appears it is necessary to refer to assessments in earlier or later years to avoid confusing landowners with tenant farmers. Another possible pitfall in the use of the assessments is the fact that they were sometimes drawn up annually and sometimes quarterly. In the case of the annual assessment the sum paid would appear to be four times the quarterly rate. This can be very misleading when comparing the assessments of one parish with those of another, or for the same parish over a period of time.

In 1798 the tax was fixed at four shillings in the pound and made a permanent charge on the land, and proprietors were given the option to redeem at fifteen years purchase. By the end of 1815 about one-third of the land was redeemed, and assessors became less interested in the owners of redeemed land. Consequently, the names of the latter began to disappear from some of the assessments. In such instances the assessments no longer represent a comprehensive record of the owners and occupiers of the land in the parish, and their value to the historian is, therefore, somewhat reduced. The practice of assessors, however, appears to have varied a good deal from parish to parish. In Leicestershire, for example, there was nearly always a separate list for exonerated land in the assessment, and the assessors continued to write in meticulously the names of owners and occupiers long since exonerated.

A more serious difficulty in the use of the assessments lies in the fact that the land tax was paid on some offices of profit, on tithes and on some buildings as well as on land. In the earlier returns, at least, the items on which the assessments were made were not always specified. This snag can partly be overcome, however, since it is often possible to deduce the payments on tithes when the payer was described as 'Rev' or 'expropriator'. In the assessment for Ripple reproduced above the payment by the Rev. Mr. Philpot was probably for the tithes. In assessments drawn up between 1825 and 1832 a more detailed description of the property is usually given, and sometimes, too, the annual rent and the payments on such a property can often be traced back over the years before 1825.

Perhaps the greatest problem in the use of the assessments is that of determining what acreage, or at least what value of land, is represented by each individual assessment. In the case of individual parishes it is possible to ascertain the total acreage and to determine the average sum paid per acre. But in order to get a general picture of the pattern of landownership and farming in this period it is necessary to study the assessments for a large number of parishes and to classify the owners and occupiers according to the size of their holdings. This would present no difficulty if we could assume that any particular payment in one parish represented approximately the same area or the same value of land in another. Unfortunately, we cannot be sure that this is always the case. There is general agreement amongst historians that the burden of the land tax was heavier in some counties than in others, and that the use of the assessments for inter-county comparisons is fraught with difficulty. When comparing assessments for parishes within the same county, however, historians are on firmer ground. Even in this case there is some evidence that there were irregularities in the assessment of the tax from one parish to another and even within the same parish, although it is quite impossible to ascertain the extent of these irregularities.

More serious than irregularities in the original assessments is the fact that there was seldom any attempt to reassess the land from time to time. Some land, particularly that which underwent enclosure, rose in value during the period covered by the assessments; yet there was no corresponding rise in the amount of tax paid on such land. Thus by the end of the eighteenth century the land tax bore inequitably on the landowners in numerous parishes. This naturally reduces, though it does not entirely eliminate, the validity of comparisons between one parish and another. By the end of the third quarter of the eighteenth century the burden of tax on each parish was fixed so that when waste or common land was taken into cultivation the burden of the land tax would be lightened.

A further difficulty arises when the assessments are used to arrange the occupying owners and tenants into categories according to the amounts they pay. It should be remembered that owners and tenants sometimes had land in more than one parish, and, therefore, it would be unwise to draw very firm lines between the different categories since a small man in one parish may be a large one in another. Similarly an owner in one parish may appear as a tenant in another or even in the same parish. This does not mean that the assessments should be discarded altogether as a source of enquiry on the much-debated problem of the 'disappearance of the small landowners'. On the contrary, they remain an essential guide to the moving picture of land distribution in any given village during the period of violent price fluctuations from 1780 to 1830.

It would be wrong to leave the reader of this short guide with the impression of overwhelming difficulties in the use of the land tax assessments. They do not lend themselves to precise quantitative analysis, but they cannot be ignored in the study of land distribution. For the village historian concerned with family histories they are of the greatest importance; and so long as the student realizes that the amounts paid cannot with any degree of certainty be equated with acreage and that a proportion — perhaps only a small proportion — of both owners and tenants were paying in more than one parish, he can make useful generalizations about the structure of rural society during a period of rapid agrarian and industrial change.

Bibliography

Chambers, J D, 'Enclosure and the Small Landowner', *Economic History Review* X (1940)

Davies, E, 'The Small Landowner, 1780-1832 in the Light of the Land Tax Assessments' *Economic History Review* I (1927)

Grigg, D B, 'The Land Tax Returns', *Agricultural History Review* XI (1963)

Hunt, H G, 'Landownership and Enclosure, 1750-1830', *Economic History Review* 2nd series, XI, (1958-9)

Johnson, A H, *The Disappearance of the Small Landowner* (Oxford, 1909). New edition with Introduction by Joan Thirsk, 1963

Martin, J M, 'Landownership and the Land Tax Returns', *Agricultural History Review 14,* 1966, pp 96-103

Mingay, G E, 'The Land Tax Assessments and the Small Landowner', *Economic History Review*, 2nd Series, XVII, 1964

Payne, E O, *Property in Land in South Bedfordshire 1750-1832* (Bedfordshire Historical Record Society, 1946)

Ward, W R, *The English Land Tax in the Eighteenth Century* (Oxford, 1953)

Parliamentary Surveys

S C Newton

[Extract from PRO Series 317/Stafford,38 Survey of the Manor of Newcastle under Lyme, 1650. Abbreviations extended]

A Survey of the Manour of New Castle under Lyne als' Lyme with the Rightes, Members and appurtenances there of lyinge and being in the County of Stafford, late parcell of the possessions of Charles Stewart, late Kinge of England, in Right of the Dutchie of Lancaster, made and taken by us whose Names are hereunto subscribed in the Moneth of June One Thousand six hundred and fifty by vertue of a Commission graunted upon an Act of the Commons assembled in Parliament for Sale of the Honours, Mannours and Landes heretofore belonginge to the late Kinge, Queene and Prince under the handes and seales of five or more of the Trustees in the said Act named and appointed. The quitt Rentes due from the Tennantes to the Lord of the aforesaid Manour of New Castle under Lyne holding of the said Manour in ffree Soccage according to the Custome thereof and payable at Michaelmas only are per annum vi^{li} xix^s ii^d

The Rentes due from the Coppyholders of the Towneshipp of Penckhull holding by ffynes certaine (according to a Decree of the Dutchie Court hereafter recyted) payable at the ffeast of Thannunciacion and St. Michael Tharchangell are per annum x^{li} oj^s xi^d

....

Ralph Sneyd esq. holdeth by Lease the perquisittes and proffites of the Courte of the said Manour vizt., waifes, estrays, goodes and chattels of felons, fugitives, Deodandes the ffarefees and Heriotes expressed in the said Decree (All fynes of the Customary Tenantes for theire Customary Lands excepted) for the yearly rent of five pounds. All which was presented by the Jury upon oath but his Lease beinge not produced wee referr it unto further Consideracion.

(Different hand) These ffynes there excepted are vallued by the Surveyours Communibus Annis lx^s

William Webb 1653

Memorandum that the perquisites etc., as aforesaid are not valuable above the Reserved Rent with the Royalties of ffishings, ffoulinges and the rest apperteninent thereunto being Included and granted by his said Leases.

Origin

A Parliamentary Survey is any inquiry into the nature and value of estates and perquisites undertaken on the authority of the House of Commons *per se* in the period 1646 to 1660. The term has come to be applied especially to the series of Surveys of Crown, Bishops' and Dean and Chapter lands made prior to their sale for the benefit of the Commonwealth.

On 9 October 1646 the estates of English bishops were vested in trustees who were to have surveys made and arrange for the selling of the property. Dean and Chapter estates were added on 30 April 1649 and on 16 July of the same year an ordinance set up an organization for the sale of Crown Lands charging part of them with £600,000 for the payment of the Army. The method of dealing with the latter types of estates was an interesting innovation. Whereas in the case of Bishops' estates the Surveys had been designed to be conducted by the traditional method of a local jury making a sworn testimony before a body of commissioners appointed to take depositions in a Court of Survey, an additional elaborate administrative machine was set up to deal with Crown and Dean and Chapter lands. This consisted of a Surveyor-General (Colonel William Webb), thirteen trustees, in whose hands the properties were placed for sale, twelve contractors, a comptroller, two registrars and four treasurers. The trustees selected the surveyors for each county and were empowered to insist that local officials should give them assistance. The Surveys themselves were drawn up according to strict rules and a model 'A Survey of the Imaginary Manor of Sale ... ' was prepared. The completed documents were returned to the registrar in duplicate and were then passed to the Surveyor-General who decided whether or not they were sufficiently accurate to serve as a basis for the sales. Webb possessed a sardonic vein of humour to which he gave full vent in his marginal comments and interlineations on inadequate Surveys.

Format

Parliamentary Surveys have a characteristic and easily recognized format. The pages are brief-size, fastened Exchequer style, written carefully (erasure was expressly forbidden) in the customary Mixed Hand of the mid seventeenth century. Overall size varies from a single page to the 'Spalding giant'(E 317 Lincoln 32) consisting of 816 folios. For Crown Land Surveys the heading is invariably in inverted pyramid form but a rectangular heading was used for fee farms and ecclesiastical property. The vast majority of Surveys were made between 1649 and 1653, the only two notable exceptions being the Forest of Needwood and Enfield Chase to which special conditions attached.

The information recorded includes the value of demesne lands, copyhold rents, customary dues, perquisites of courts, particulars of chief rents, fines and leases, tithes, timber and wastes. An abstract of the whole was drawn up and the Surveys conclude with the jurors' signatures, where appropriate, and the Surveyors' signed certificate of correctness, countersigned by Webb. Maps and plans are not often found; where bounds were likely to cause confusion, notably in open fields, the surveyors were instructed to provide strict delineation by reference to adjacent parcels. Speed was an important consideration and as a result elaborate measurement was forbidden.

Location

Considerable confusion has arisen by misapprehension of what constitutes an 'original' Survey and the problem is too complicated to be elaborated here. The following is merely an indication as to the whereabouts of main series.

Dean and Chapter Surveys are frequently found among capitular archives and those of Bishops' lands were sometimes sent to the respective diocese, the decision being left to the Archbishop of Canterbury in 1662. The remainder were deposited at Lambeth Palace where they still are, but a number of ecclesiastical surveys are to be found in the House of Lords Record Office and the British Museum. For Crown lands the Public Record Office is the chief repository of Surveys. The bulk are in the Exchequer (Augmentation Office) Series (E 317) with a partially duplicating Series, a few with maps, among the records of the Land Revenue Office (L.R.2). A third series consists mainly of transcripts of those relating to the Duchy of Lancaster estates (D.L.32). Extracts and, occasionally, full transcripts were made and these often survive in County Record Offices and other local repositories, among private estate collections.

Uses of Parliamentary Surveys and Future Research

One of the major advantages of this type of record is its completeness, both in coverage and comprehensiveness. Virtually every Crown or ecclesiastical property in all the counties of England and Wales was included, although the number of Surveys naturally depends on the relative distribution of the different types of ownership. For example Middlesex has 99 concerned with Crown Land, Durham and Northumberland only 16 between them. The kinds of property dealt with are diverse; manors, fee farms, burgage tenements, even the underground workings of a coal mine are included. Detailed accounts of houses and other buildings sometimes occur (occasionally architectural descriptions). The quantities of demesne land, annual values, the level of rents, revenue from feudal dues, and the profits of timber are all ascertainable. The accounts given of leases are valuable indications of the policy of the Crown and ecclesiastical landlords on this important question and the Surveys also indicate the 'disappearance' of Church lands and tithes. Since the surveyors were primarily concerned with market rather than nominal value and with actual profitability rather than with customary feudal dues, a more realistic idea of the wealth, actual and potential, of Church and State can be obtained. In addition information of importance for local history, such as local office-holders, field-names and topographical details can be found. Occasionally genealogical purposes are served in the particulars of tenants and the descent of their holdings. The accuracy of the Surveys, particularly those of Crown and Dean and Chapter lands, makes them an invaluable standard for assessing subsequent alterations. In some cases the work was so well done and the succeeding changes so few that a Survey was used for practical purposes long after it was made. This happened, for example, with the Needwood Forest Survey of 1658 which was used as the basis for the proposed enclosure of 1778. In 1775 a decision of Exchequer Chamber gave Parliamentary Surveys complete judicial recognition.

Much more needs to be known about the success or failure of the land sales, the methods of producing and meeting the cost of the Surveys, and the surveyors themselves, notably Webb, who surely deserves at least a monograph. Apart from S. J. Madge's account of the Crown land sales no work has been done on the administrative background. The value of Parliamentary

Surveys is such that it is unfortunate that very few have been printed *in extenso*, and most of those that have been were published in the nineteenth century.

Bibliography

Madge, S J, *The Domesday of Crown Lands* (1938) A detailed account of the sale of Crown estates and the politics and administration behind it.

Newton, S C, 'Parliamentary Surveys of the Hundreds of Appletree and Gresley', *Derbyshire Archaeological Journal*, LXXXI (1961) Transcript, with introduction, of a characteristic example.

Public Record Office, *Lists and Indexes*, XXV (1908) Lists all the Surveys in the Augmentation Office series.

Wilian,T S, 'Parliamentary Surveys for the North Riding of Yorkshire', *Yorkshire Archaeological Journal*, part 123 (1933). Examines the kind of evidence provided by the Surveys.

Turnpike Records

Baron F Duckham

[Record Office for Cumberland, Westmorland and the City of Carlisle: 1st Minute Book of Carlisle to Brampton Turnpike Trust]

Great Jury Room, Carlisle
4th Oct. 1828

At a meeting of the Trustees held here this day.

Present: Revd. Tho. Ramshay, Chairman [and eight other trustees,named]

Ord^d.   That the Estimate of John Milburn of Great Corby, Mason, for building a new Bridge over the Cairn and making additions to the old one on the road leading from Carlisle to Brampton by Warwick [Bridge] for the sum of £245 be accepted and taken up on the proper Securities being given by him.

Ord^d.   That when the Arch of Gelt Bridge is turned to the Satisfaction of the Surveyor and the Bridge Master the Committee be empowered to direct the Treasurer to pay the Contractors £144 on acct. of the work.

Odr^d.   That Messrs Tho. Hilton & Armstrong be the Contractors for building the new Toll House at Botcherby Bridge for the Sum of £102.

Ord^d.   That Messrs Hodgson & How have £10 advanced to them on Acct. of the railing between Middle Gelt Bridge and Brampton on Condition that they complete the whole work by 11 November.

Ord^d.   That the Accounts of the Treasurer, Clerk & Surveyor having been examined and compared with the Vouchers be allowed & passed.

Balance in the Hands of the Treasurer £732—18—9. ...

Origin

The turnpiking of stretches of highway from 1663 until about the fourth decade of the nineteenth century was an attempt to force the road user rather than solely the local inhabitants to bear the chief cost of road improvement and maintenance. Although the principle of levying tolls for such purposes was not entirely new, it was only in the eighteenth century that it became a common practice. Trusts were established by individual Acts of Parliament, normally for twenty-one years, and were in most cases renewed by subsequent Acts until the mid or late nineteenth century. By then the phenomenal development of rail transport and the accumulated mortgage debts had rendered the majority of trusts quite insolvent, while the ubiquitous toll gate became an ever greater public annoyance. The turnpikes of South Wales were abolished under an Act of 1844 and the roads handed over to County Road Boards. Elsewhere trusts were usually allowed to expire naturally before the highways in their care became the responsibility of Boroughs, Highway Districts, Sanitary Boards, or (ultimately) County Councils. The last trust ended in 1895.

Format and Location

The local records of turnpike trusts consist of Acts, deeds, minute books, accounts and balance sheets, vouchers, correspondence and miscellaneous items such as the reports of the trustees' surveyor, occasional contracts for work, maps, and a few printed handbills. Only rarely have the individual toll bar accounts kept by the collectors survived. The printed copies of a trust's Act(s) are often among these records, sometimes inside the front cover of a minute book. Some may also be in local reference libraries. The minute books are generally folio-type volumes whose earlier entries are likely to be among the most informative. Since trustees transacted largely routine business once the road was completed, it is by no means unusual to find that three or four minute books cover the life-span of trusts even of some longevity. The accounts will also often be in ledger form, though balance sheets — giving an abstract of income, expenditure and indebtedness — may frequently be discovered amongst the minutes. The remaining papers will be almost wholly in boxes or bundles.

The happiest hunting ground for all these classes of document is the County Record Office [C.R.O.]. Unfortunately there was no standard or automatic procedure for the disposal of documents at the winding up of a trust. Many records have undoubtedly perished, though a few may still lie with the firms of country solicitors which originally acted as the trusts' clerks. In Scotland many miscellaneous records (including a few minute books) will also be found in the Scottish Record Office, Register House, Edinburgh.

Uses of Turnpike Trust Records

The documents will be most useful for reconstructing the history of a particular trust, but they can also throw light on other matters.

As is widely recognized, the involvement of country gentlemen in transport undertakings was profound. Careful inspection of the extant records in the C.R.O. will help to elucidate the degree of participation of the local landed families in turnpike development and demonstrate how far such connections were mainly in promotion, administration or investment. Turnpike Acts normally mention the original trustees by name (occasionally over two hundred of them!) but only research in the minute and account books themselves will reveal the true picture. Few trustees attended meetings once the first flush of excitement was past and minute books often record the cancellation or postponement of business because a quorum could not be obtained. Thus the existence of a large number of titled trustees may only mean that the trust sought to impress prospective investors with its respectability and credit-worthiness. A rather more sophisticated use to which the records might be put would be to compile a list of the toll receipts or toll gate leases for a group of contiguous trusts over a series of years. This in itself could help to tell us much about the level of regional domestic trade, especially when linked to the revenue statistics from local waterways.

Finally a large amount of information about the techniques and standard of contemporary road making can be derived from the minute books and (more particularly) from the correspondence of the Clerk of the Trust and from surveyors' reports. Turnpike engineering has received an almost uniformly bad press from both contemporaries and historians, but standards clearly varied enormously. Some trusts remained content with the appointment of unskilled surveyors of no great competence. Others, mainly after the first decade of the nineteenth century, increasingly sought the services of men with practical training, and some famous road engineers were appointed surveyors. The accounts of some trusts are full enough for a surprising amount of detail concerning costs of labour and materials to emerge.

Ancillary Records and Their Use

The official documents will often tell one comparatively little about the turnpike's initial promotion, while gaps in the records may be partially off-set by reference to these other sources. Local newspaper files, often obtainable in the reference library of the nearest large town, are invaluable. Advertisements were used to call interested parties together to discuss promotion and elect a committee to prepare the Bill for Parliament. Some newspapers commented on such schemes in their editorials. Once established, trusts normally leased their toll gates (either singly or severally) to the highest bidder(s). Where the early accounts are defective or missing the local newspaper can usually be of help. The periodic auctioning of toll bars would be duly advertised and the terms of the previous lease noted. Some lessees became virtually professional toll farmers with their activities extending over more than one region. The names of a few of the greatest occur in the minutes of evidence of Parliamentary Select Committees. By painstaking use of the files the income of the trustees can be recovered for quite long periods. From 1822 turnpike accounts had to be deposited with the Clerk of the Peace and copies may be found in the County Quarter Sessions records.

Much information on turnpikes in fact exists in the Parliamentary Papers (see **Powell, W R,** *Local History from Blue Books* (Historical Association 1962). The principal reports and minutes of evidence will be found listed in **Ford P** and **G,** *Hansard's Catalogue and Breviate of Parliamentary Papers 1696-1834* and the same authors' *Select List of British Parliamentary Papers 1833-1899* (both 1953). The *Journals of the House of Commons* and *Lords,* available in the better libraries, permit one to trace the stages of many turnpike Bills and also note petitions filed for and against them.

It is also worth seeing whether the records of rival transport undertakings contain any references. Frequently a search in the minute books of a nearby canal or early railway company will reveal a few details which otherwise would go unnoticed. Similarly the reports of engineers to railway promotion committees sometimes include an estimate of the amount of traffic to be tapped — with a consequent assessment of the business of the local turnpikes. The vast majority of railway and canal documents are open to public inspection at the British Transport Historical Records Offices in London (66 Porchester Road,

Turnpike Records
W.2), York and Edinburgh. The private papers of landed families form another vital source of information and the student should always try to trace the personal archives of the more important trustees. Large collections of such papers are held by most C.R.O.s, some City Archives Departments or, in the case of Scotland, Register House, Edinburgh. Old estate plans and maps for counties or regions are also in the possession of these offices and are of obvious importance. Inquiry should be made for the original turnpike plans which had, from 1792, to be deposited with the Clerks of the Peace. Last of all, one should not forget to examine the physical record on the ground: toll houses, milestones and so forth.

Bibliography

The background and organisation of turnpikes is well described in **Jackman, W T**, *The Development of Transportation in Modern England* (3rd ed. with introduction by W H Chaloner, 1966) and **Webb, S** and **B**, *The Story of the King's Highway* (1913, repr. 1963).
The following give information on the handling of literary or physical evidence, or are useful as model studies:
Cossons, A, *Turnpike Roads of Nottinghamshire* (Hist. Assoc., 1934)
Cox, C and **Surry, N**, 'The Archaeology of Turnpike Roads', *J. of Industrial Archaeology*, II, 1 (1965)
Emmison, F G, 'Turnpike Roads and Toll Gates of Bedfordshire' *Beds. Hist. Rec. Soc. Survey Series,* vol. III, 1936)
Emmison, F G and **Gray, I**, *County Records* (Hist. Assoc., rev. ed., 1961)
French, E C W, 'Turnpike Trusts', *The Amateur Historian*, II, 1 (1954)
MacMahon, K A, *Roads and Turnpike Trusts in Eastern Yorkshire* (E. Yorks Local Hist. Soc., 1964)
Meickle, W P, 'Highway Repairs in the Eighteenth Century' *Trans Newcomen Soc.* XXI (1940-41)
Russell, P, *A Leicestershire Road* (1934)
Wilson, R G, 'Transport Dues as Indices of Economic Growth 1775-1820', *Econ. Hist.Rev.* 2nd series, XIX, 1 (1966)
Many contemporary writings are also relevant. See especially:
McAdam, J L, *Remarks on the Present System of Roadmaking ...* (1816)
Parnell, Sir Henry, *A Treatise on Roads* (1833)
Scott, John, *Digests of the General Highway and Turnpike Laws* (1778)

Fire Insurance Policy Registers

J H Thomas

[Extract from Sun Fire Register Ms. 11,936/266, Guildhall Library, by kind permission of the Sun Alliance and London Insurance Group.]

ditto

399036	William Fairchild of Sawston in the County of Cambridge Merchant on his	
£6.1.	Buildings Goods and Stock as Particularly described on the Back of this Policy Vis	
Mid 1779	On his household Goods in his now dwelling House	
£6.8.6.	only situate as aforesaid Timber and Tiled not exceeding Two hundred Pounds	200
	Utensils and Stock Vis In the Great Barn seperate not exceeding One Hundred and Twenty Pounds	120
	In the small Barn not exceeding Fifty Pounds	50
	In a House adjoining the Stable not exceeding Thirty Pounds	30
	In the Stack Yard only not exceeding One hundred Pounds	100
	In Two Paper Mills adjoining in the Parish aforesaid Timber and Tiled not exceeding Six Hundred and Seventy five Pounds	675
	In Three Warehouses adjoining not exceeding Two Hundred and Thirty Pounds	230
	the following in Little Abington in the County aforesaid in the tenure of John Butcher or his Undertenants	
	House only not exceeding Two hundred Pounds	200
	Bakehouse and Dairy adjoining not exceeding Thirty five Pounds	35
	Barns Stables Hogsties and Waggon Lodge adjoining not exceeding Eighty Pounds	80
	Barn and Cartlodge adjoining not exceeding Seventy five Pounds	75
	Cowhouse Stable Henhouse and Hogsties adjoining not exceeding Forty Pounds	40
	House and Bakehouse adjoining not exceeding One Hundred Pounds	100

Carried forward £1935

Origin

Prior to the eighteenth century the insurance of property against fire had been conducted in a very piecemeal fashion. Business was usually conducted in two ways, either as a personal venture by one or two individuals or as a plan of mutual contribution. It was not until 1710 that the first fully organised fire insurance concern appeared, the first meeting of the managers of the Sun Fire Office taking place in Causey's Coffee House not far from St. Paul's. The idea of eliminating at least a part of the risk of fire soon spread, and within ten years another three major companies had been formed. In 1717 the Westminster Fire Office opened for business, the Royal Exchange and London Assurance both following in 1720. Though London offered the largest potential market for fire insurance concerns, the idea was by no means confined to the Metropolis, and by 1790 Fire Offices had been opened at Worcester, Bath and Leeds.

While the network of fire offices slowly grew, their method of conducting business was of a standard type. In return for paying a premium the client received a policy, the details of which were entered in the company's registers. Whereas only a few individual policies still exist from those early days, the duplicate registers are fairly numerous.

Format and Location

Fire policy registers are, for the most part, stoutly bound ledgers, some complete with a strap across the spine to permit ease of carriage. (A major exception to this is the Supplemental Agents' series of the Royal Exchange Assurance; in this case, entries were made by local agents on printed pages and despatched to the head office in London, where they were pasted into a ledger.) The register entries, written in a variety of hands, range in length from two to three lines to several pages as happened when the London Dock Company insured all its property in 1840 for £150,000.

The details recorded include the date and number of the policy, a description of the property, the amount for which the policy was being taken out, and the rate. For a lengthy entry, a running total was included, usually to the right of the register page. The way in which these details were set out varied from one company to another. Thus the pages of Sun Fire registers are divided into three columns, while those of the Royal Exchange Assurance are divided into four. Where several policies were issued on the same day, as happened more and more with the increase in business, 'ditto' was placed at the start of each subsequent entry. Thus William Fairchild's policy was actually taken out on 2 June 1779. Additional information to be found on the register pages includes the date when the policy was to fall due, the name of the agent who issued it, sometimes by place and sometimes by personal name, and whether or no the policy was replacing an older one. Many of the entries in Sun Fire registers conclude with two or three names, usually those of company officials.

The location of old policy registers can easily be found via a letter to the firm concerned. In some cases they have been deposited in the Guildhall Library,

London. Some 1,200 volumes of registers of the Sun Fire Company, covering the period 1710-1860, are to be found there, along with registers for the Royal Exchange and London Assurance concerns. In other cases, Phoenix Assurance for example, the registers remain in the care of the parent company, where they may be consulted on request. The major drawback to searching policy registers is that they are usually unindexed, though the policy entries are set out in chronological order. On the brighter side of things, the Guildhall Library does have detailed schedules, covering dates of volumes and policy numbers, and runs a very good photocopying service for lengthier entries.

The Use of Fire Policy Registers

The value of old fire policy registers goes far beyond that of mere curiosity. Initially, they show who actually owned a certain piece of property and whether, as the illustration above shows, all or part of it was being leased out. Just as important as the name of the person taking out the policy is his or her occupation. Here fire policy registers are of particular value, in that they shed direct light on a common occurrence of former times — the combining of several occupations by one man. The example shows that Fairchild followed at least two occupations — those of merchant and farmer— as well as owning two paper mills. Evidence of this nature is of obvious importance to both economic and local historians.

Besides giving information on the combining of occupations, fire insurance policy registers also give some indication of the relative wealth and standard of living of the persons taking out policies. Thus the policy for £400 taken out by a Middlesex lawyer in 1778 included books to the value of £40 and plate for a similar sum. Where a business or industrial concern was being insured, further conclusions may be drawn as to the relative prosperity of the concern; in the case of combined occupations, it is possible to work out which was the more reliable in terms of income or to at least draw some inferences.

As many industrial concerns, particularly mills, were insured against the risk of fire, the old registers will be of use to the industrial historian as well as his local and economic counterparts. He will be able to gain much valuable evidence about the scale of plant used in these early industrial enterprises. Where several policies were taken out on the same concern over a fair space of time, the industrial historian may well discover that an increase in plant took place, sufficient evidence in itself of an increase in the demand for a product, and of resultant increased prosperity. Thus Henry Portal, Hampshire's famous paper-maker, insured his house, mill and outhouses at Laverstoke for £300 in 1719; eight years later the same property, plus storehouses and raghouses, was insured for £1,200. In 1742, Portal took out a third policy, to cover the same property and 'one other little paper mill', for £2,000.

While giving some idea of the scale of plant, in the case of a mill, fire insurance registers occasionally shed some light on the type of plant used. When James Sharp insured his windmill at Stanstead in 1829, the policy was to include 'Sacks, Ropes, Straps, Flour Cloths, Dressing Machines and other Articles in use'. Similarly, when Mary Streater insured her paper mill at Bramshott, Hampshire, in 1725, the policy was to cover 'the Wheels Hammers Engines and other Utensils in the said Mills'.

As well as the scale and type of plant, fire policy registers often give the site of the building or buildings being insured in relation to others nearby. When James Clark, a London shoemaker, took out a policy with the Sun Fire Office in April, 1727, he was described as being 'at the Corner of Coleman Street next London Wall in the parish of St Stephen'. Details are occasionally given of exact distances. A register entry for 1739 tells us that a paper-maker's house was situated some seven yards from his mill. The value of such evidence is obvious, since parish Tithe maps date only from 1836 onwards.

A final point of importance is that register entries often give some indication of the outlets for industrial and other products. Thus the fact that an eighteenth-century Hampshire merchant insured a warehouse at Chichester and a cornmill at nearby Nutbourn suggests that he was shipping corn out through the port of Chichester. Similarly, the insuring of a Thames-side warehouse by a paper-maker from N.E. Hampshire suggests, very strongly, that he was sending the output from his mill to London. Commodities as well as property were insured and in this respect fire policy registers are of particular use to the economic historian. Diligent searching will be rewarded with, amongst other things, much valuable evidence about the tonnage of ships in the eighteenth and nineteenth centuries and the spread of agricultural machinery in the nineteenth. Used in conjunction with early directories, maps and other evidence, fire insurance policy registers form a useful source of additional information for the researcher, a source that is all too often overlooked.

Bibliography

Baumer, E, *Early Days of the Sun Fire Office* (London, 1910)

Dickson, P G M, *The Sun Insurance Office, 1710-1960* (Oxford, 1960)

Raynes, H E, *A History of British Insurance* (2nd edition, Pitman, 1964)

Relton, F B, *An Account of the Fire Insurance Companies ... including the Sun Fire Office; also of Charles Povey* (Sonnenschein, 1893)

Scott, W R, *Constitution and Finance of English, Scottish and Irish joint Stock Companies to 1720* (Cambridge University Press, 3 vols. 1910-2)

Street, G S, *The London Assurance, 1720-1920* (London, 1920)

Tithe Apportionments and Maps

Lionel M Munby

'Whereas an Agreement for the Commutation of Tithes in the parish of Rampton in the County of Cambridge was, on the Sixth Day of August in the Year One Thousand Eight Hundred and Forty two, confirmed by the Tithe Commissioners for England and Wales, of which Agreement, with the Schedule thereunto annexed, the following is a Copy:

Articles of Agreement ... made and executed at a parochial meeting of Landowners and Titheowners ... By and Between the several persons Owners of Land within the said parish ... and the Interest of which Landowners in the lands of the said parish is not less than two thirds of the lands therein subject to tithes of the one part and ... the Estate of the Reverend John Fowler Clerk a Lunatic Rector of the said parish and owner of all the tithes thereof of the other parts
It is hereby agreed that the annual sum of Three hundred Pounds ... shall be paid to ... the Estate ... and to the Successors of the said John Fowler in the said Rectory instead of all the tithes of the lands within the said parish ... and instead of all Moduses and Compositions real and prescriptive and customary payments ... and ... all Easter Offerings payable by or in respect of any of the Inhabitants of the said parish ...'

[The Schedule opens with a summary table of the acreages of woodland and of arable, meadow or pasture, both enclosed and in the open field. This is followed by the Tithe Commissioners' apportionment of the 'rent charge amongst the lands of the said parish', of which an extract follows:]

Landowners	Occupiers	Numbers referring to the Plan	Name and description of Lands and Premises	State of Cultivation	Quantities in statute Measure		
					A.	R.	P.
Asplen William	Himself	108	Allotment in Little Field	Arable	6	2	17
Aworth Mary	Herself	148	House Homestead and Garden	—	,,	3	4
	Ingle Henry and Smith Thomas	25	Allotment in Nether Irams	Pasture	3	1	20
		26	do.　　　do.	do.	7	1	13
		150	Home Close	do.	1	2	13
					12	1	6

'There are Thirty six Commonable Houses or Scites of Commonable Houses in the said parish of Rampton to each of which is attached one Common right
The owner of each Common right is entitled to turn Four Cows upon the Commons

Tithe Apportionments and Maps

Meadows and Fields of Rampton and to an unlimited right of Keeping Sheep over the same
The undermentioned lands in the said parish have been immemorially tithe free — that is to say Mowing Commons'

[The names of owners and occupiers, and the acreage follow, and the complete schedule of the Apportionment is attached to a large-scale map, on which each property is numbered.]

Origin

The obligation to pay tithe, one tenth of all produce, to the Rector and Vicar, and after the Reformation to lay Rectors where they existed, led to endless friction in a farming community. Diocesan and parochial archives contain many documents which reveal the difficulties of collecting so complex a tax in kind. There are occasional records of attempts by the Tithe owner to obtain an agreed commutation into a money payment. In some cases parliamentary enclosure was used to commute tithe. In 1836 a Tithe Commutation Act was passed, under which a body of Tithe Commissioners was set up to supervise the commutation of Tithe wherever it was still paid in kind. For the great majority of parishes a large-scale plan and accompanying schedule of apportionment was drawn up. This was necessary in order to fix the exact money obligation of each piece of property. In fact the Commissioners produced 'a General Survey and Register of Real Property' during the late 1830s and early 1840s.

Location and Format

Three copies of each plan and apportionment were made. One was deposited with the Incumbent and may still be found in the Vestry or in a loft or in the Rectory. It is often missed because it is so large. It is easy to mistake the huge tin container of some Tithe Commutation plans for part of an old-fashioned central heating system! A second copy was deposited with the Diocesan Registrar, and a third was kept by the Tithe Commissioners. Either or both of the first two copies may now be in the County Record Office or other repository. The Tithe Commissioners' copies are now in the Public Record Office and stored in the Branch Repository at Ashridge, Herts. The Tithe Redemption Office, East Block, Barrington Road, Worthing, Sussex has microfilm copies.

The Tithe plans are nearly all huge but there is no single standard scale. They are of varying reliability (see Harley, *op. cit.*, in Bibliography). Some use colours, for example dwellings in red and other buildings in grey. They show greens and commons, and often miniature drawings of windmills; post mills and tower mills can be distinguished. Each property is numbered; manorial waste is distinguished by having no plot number. The Apportionment consists of an opening 'Articles of Agreement', as in the Rampton example, followed by the Schedule divided into eight columns. The first contains the landowners listed alphabetically; the second the occupiers, either the landowner, as 'himself' or a named tenant. The third column contains a number referring to the plan. Because the properties are listed in alphabetical order of landowners, these numbers occur in no clear order. The surveyors seem simply to have numbered properties on the ground, as they came to them. It is therefore best to work from the Apportionment to the plan.

The fourth column contains a 'name and description' of the property; in most Apportionments this is a primary source for field names; farm and house names, and in some cases field names are not given. The fifth column gives the 'state of cultivation', a primary source for the study of land use, but limited in value because the nature of the crop is not indicated. The sixth gives the acreage, in acres, roods, and perches (40 perches = 1 rood; 4 roods = 1 acre). The seventh column contains the rent-charge in lieu of tithe, and the eighth is for 'Remarks'; these two columns have been omitted from the extract printed above.

At the end of the Schedule is a 'Summary' of the total acreages of each landowner and occupier. It saves time to use this summary when calculating parochial totals, instead of working through the whole Schedule, but it may be necessary to check back for more information in the case of the 'occupiers'.

Finally there may be some important, additional information such as appears in the Rampton Apportionment, where enclosure was taking place *pari passu* with the Tithe Apportionment. In the preamble to the Schedule there may be references to tithe free lands; in some cases these give the extent of a monastic estate at the Dissolution.

The Uses of Tithe Documents

Two things make these documents invaluable: the fact that this information is readily available in so many parishes and for much the same date; and the detailed knowledge which can be obtained about each piece of real property. The best way to make use of the information is to map it onto modern OS 6" maps (25" for built-up areas) in a series of traces. A traced map of field boundaries with names and acreages, approximately accurate for some 130 years ago, is an invaluable tool from which research can go backwards or forwards. This can be used to locate properties mentioned in rentals, leases and title deeds. The location of early open fields can be roughly assessed. Where the Tithe Apportionment was made before enclosure, as in counties of late enclosure like Cambridge, we have detailed information about the open field system. In such cases there was usually a later Altered Apportionment, after enclosure, from which useful comparative information can be obtained. Such Altered Apportionments also exist for areas in which there was substantial urbanisation.

Maps of field boundaries, farm boundaries and 'estate' boundaries will be most useful for forward comparison. As J T Coppock has suggested (*op. cit.* in Bibliography) both field and farm boundaries have changed in the last century and a half much more often than is popularly supposed. Using the Tithe plan as a base one can follow these changes, piecemeal in sales documents and comprehensively in the editions of large scale Ordnance Survey Maps. In urban areas early railway lines and industrial developments can be mapped.

A final trace map of land use can be made, with which the Dudley Stamp Land Use Survey of the 1930s and the one now in progress can be compared. The biggest problem in using the Tithe Apportionments to map land use arises from the 'arable and pasture' description. Does this mean a piece of land part of which was arable, part pasture, or an area of ley farming? One's suspicion is that pasture usually means permanent or apparently permanent pasture, and arable all ploughed land; while the two together usually imply a piece of land cultivated in two ways in different parts. Land use is in any case difficult to define as the contemporary land use survey is revealing; the Tithe Apportionment information is only a general guide, but it is nevertheless much more revealing than anything else we have so early.

Most of this information can be summarised statistically as well as mapped, and useful comparisons, in detail and in general, can be made with the 1841 and 1851 Census Returns. For example a farmer of X acres employing Y men in the census may be identifiable in the Tithe Apportionment and so the location of his farm be discovered.

The comprehensive list of land occupiers in the Tithe Apportionment can be used to follow changes in farm occupation, backwards in rentals and other estate records, forwards in local Directories. The occupation of farms probably changed quite as much as their boundaries. How did villages differ in these respects? Why was there more continuity in some places than in others? These are the kinds of questions which local research can often answer.

Bibliography

Return of all Tithes Commuted and Apportioned under the Acts for Commutation of Tithes (British Sessional Papers, House of Commons, 1887, vol. LXIV, pp. 239-533).

Coppock, J T, 'Changes in Farm and Field Boundaries in the Nineteenth Century', in *The Amateur Historian,* Vol.3, no.7.

Prince, H C, 'The Tithe Surveys of the Mid-Nineteenth Century' in *The Agricultural History Review* vol. VII (1959)

Harley, J B, 'Maps for the Local Historian — A Guide to British Sources: 3. Enclosure and Tithe Maps' *The Amateur Historian,* vol.7, no. 8, to be reprinted in pamphlet form. This contains a considerable bibliography.

Chapter Act Books

Shelagh Bond

[Extracts from the chapter act book, 1672 -1684, of the College of Windsor, VI.B.4, preserved in the Aerary, St. George's Chapel.]

July the 7th 1679.
Present in the chapter house Dr Durel Dean, Dr Fulham, Dr Evans, Dr Milward, Dr Buttler.
Ordered that the Supporters about the Kings arms on the Poor Knights houses of the New foundation, which have been long standing there by inadvertence, those supporters being those of Oliver Cromwell's sett up there in the time of his usurpation, be cutt down and defaced.
Ordered that the Lord Chamberlains letter of June the 3d, where his Lordship acknowledges the Priviledge of this Church, in having no body putt upon them to lodge in their houses, be registred....
July the 24th [16]79
Present in the chapter house Dr Durel, Dean, Dr Fulham, Dr Buttler, Dr Scot, Dr Vossius.
Agreed that James the son of Mr John Harod of the town of New Windsor, and Thomas Hall, the grandchild of Mr Bessnet the Sexton, be admitted Quiristers of this Church for half places, their pay to beginn from the 25th currant....
[1 May 1682]
Mr Chiffinch's estate wee value at 260£ per annum de claro, but wee renew'd his lease for 3 yeares elapsd this Lady day, for 50£ hee haveing done us singular service in getting us a discharge out of the exchequor for the 48£.7s.9d. issueing to the crown from the new land rents which was claim'd for the year 1672 & severall other kindnesses.
Ordered that all work about the roof of the Church cease till further direction from Sir Christopher Wren which Mr Locumtenens is to write for to the said Sir Christopher
Ordered that the water tables of Dr Butlers house bee forthwith repaird at the College charges.
May 2 Presentibus Doctore Fulham Locumtenente, Doctoribus Hascard, Somerez, Magistro Roswell.
The quire were severely rebuked for their irreverent behaviour in the chapell at Divine service, his Majestie haveing taken notice of their misdemeanor.

The Nature of Chapter Act Books

Nine English cathedrals in the Middle Ages, York, Chichester, Exeter, Hereford, Lichfield, Lincoln, London, Salisbury and Wells, were served by colleges of secular clergy; among two hundred or more other such colleges were such well-known examples as Beverley and St. George's, Windsor. Since the Reformation the refounded monastic cathedrals have also been governed by secular chapters as have the sixteenth century foundations of Bristol, Chester, Gloucester, Oxford, Peterborough and Westminster Abbey. The composition of secular chapters varied from body to body, but each was usually headed by a provost, or a dean, recognised as 'first in session and voice, and the more honourable part of the chapter'. Meetings, held daily or weekly in the Middle Ages, have in recent centuries been less frequent. The decisions taken by the chapter, which were binding on successors and absentees, were known as *acta* and registered in chapter act books. In some cathedrals these were called minute books. Practice, however, varied. At Worcester in the eighteenth century two series of minute books and act books ran concurrently, with virtually identical entries. At Winchester, on the other hand, a separate volume (1665-1737) contained 'orders of chapter ... not proper to be formed into acts and to stand upon record in the chapter clerk's book of acts'. In medieval chapter act books, entries tended to be arranged somewhat haphazardly, or by subjects. From the sixteenth or early seventeenth century when, incidentally, Latin yielded slowly to English, *acta* were more usually registered in chronological order.

The Use of the Records

Records extending over six hundred years are unlikely to conform to any rigid pattern. Some act books contain copies of many important letters and documents; others are rich in leases; others, again, in grants of next presentations to benefices; much is of relatively minor domestic interest. Some variations derive from the range in date; probate of wills, for instance, a marked feature in the Lincoln act books until 1536, disappears there by 1547. Chapter act books of the seventeenth century seem especially detailed. Wayward omissions and irregularities, together with the inclusion of routine entries — installations, elections, protestations of canons intending to reside, to name but a few — may limit the value of certain act books at certain periods and at certain places, but there is compensation in the variety of what is entered on other occasions.

Chapter act books are an obvious starting point for any study of the institution concerned; they may well be the only source at some dates for rules of residence and for the emoluments and dividends of canons. In the sphere of church services, orders relating to preaching in the early seventeenth century yield after the Restoration to concern for the enrichment of worship; and in the nineteenth century the growing influence of the Oxford Movement can be traced in provision of more early morning Celebrations. The responsibility of chapters for discipline resulted everywhere in admonitions, with occasional lively *verbatim* examinations of recalcitrant lay clerks or bedesmen.

The wealth of personal entries in chapter act books makes them a valuable quarry for the biographer. As well as information concerning deans and canons, they furnish very full evidence for the *fasti* of lesser clergy and laymen. In fifteenth and early sixteenth century registers, for example in those of Southwell, St. Paul's and Lincoln, are to be found appointments of chantry priests; at Winchester a list of clerical and lay officers, including bedesmen and choristers, heads each general chapter. Musical historians are already using chapter act books for tracing organists, lay clerks and choristers, such as the two Windsor boys, James and Thomas, mentioned in the extract above.

Acta concerning the fabric, not only of cathedrals and their precincts, but also of the chancels of those churches which formed part of their endowment, are especially valuable when bills, plans and other papers no longer survive. Some medieval chapter act books contain such entries; and in the modern period, notably at the Restoration, chapter act books may well be the main source. Domestic architecture in the precincts was the subject of considerable expenditure in the 1660s; orders for work to be done in deans' and canons' houses may be used in conjunction with probate inventories.

Chapters held manors, lands, rectories and tithes all over the country, often far removed from the cathedral or college itself. Leases are recorded in the act books with fair completeness, and policy may be traced from *acta* limiting the term of years or laying down covenants to be included in future leases. On several occasions at Windsor after the Restoration unceremonious bargaining between chapter and tenant over fines is entered with considerable frankness, information probably recorded nowhere else. Incidental topographical detail can be gleaned from a lease of stone quarries, the grant of timber for barns, a licence to dig for coal, an order to erect a windmill or an agreement to build shops. The Winchester chapter was petitioned in 1632 by their tenants of Lower Wootton who, since the inclosure of their fields had 'been continuallie molested and much wronged' by the farmer who had taken their pasture, inclosed a large green lane, grubbed up an old hedge and planted a new one in their common. Care over valuable timber on chapter estates is often meticulous. Chapters were notorious litigants and many entries concerned their law suits. Dealings with the borough or city outside their precincts might be uneasy, as at Winchester in 1637 when a difference concerning the extent of jurisdictions and liberties is amply documented. Happier relations are implied in orders to distribute sixty groats to the poor within and without the city walls.

Some of the interest of chapter act books derives from isolated entries. There is a grant by the Salisbury chapter for a man to go on pilgrimage in 1343 and, in the sixteenth century, manumission of serfs at Lincoln and Chichester. A list of relics belonging to St. Hugh's shrine at Lincoln was compiled in 1520 and injunctions made after a legatine visit there in 1556. A poor knight of Windsor was given permission to adventure to Guyana in 1631. The miscellaneous nature of such entries makes chapter act books valuable but difficult to use; and all too few are in print. Nevertheless, their contribution in many fields is considerable and no local historian should neglect those which may relate to his town, manor or parish.

The Location of Records

In 1951 the Pilgrim Trust published a typescript *Survey of Ecclesiastical Archives*; copies are preserved in the British Museum, Lambeth Palace Library, the House of Lords Record Office, the Bodleian Library and Cambridge University Library. This lists 660 surviving chapter act books, but omits those which may have survived from now defunct medieval secular colleges. These colleges are listed in **Knowles, M D** and **Hadcock, R N,** *Medieval Religious Houses* (1953), pp. 232-346. The whereabouts of act books surviving from bodies not surveyed by the Trust may be traced through the National Register of Archives and local record offices. The chapter act books of existing colleges and cathedrals are usually preserved in the custody of the dean and canons concerned and inquiry should be made to the archivist, chapter clerk or chapter librarian.

Bibliography

Bond, Shelagh (ed), introduction by **Bond, M,** *The Chapter Acts of the Dean and Canons of Windsor, 1430, 1523 — 1672* (1966)

Chew, H M (ed), *Hemingsby's Register* [Salisbury] (1963)

Cole, R E G, *Chapter Acts of the cathedral church of St Mary of Lincoln 1520-1536* (1915); 1536-1547 (1917); 1547-1559 (1920)

Edwards, K, *The English Secular Cathedrals in the Middle Ages* (2nd ed., 1967)

Fowler, J T (ed), *Acts of Chapter of the collegiate church of SS. Peter and Wilfred, Ripon, 1452—1506* (1875)

Leach, A F (ed), *Memorials of Beverley Minster* (2 vols. 1898, 1903)

Leach, A F (ed), *Visitations and Memorials of Southwell Minster* (1891)

Peckham, W D (ed), *The Acts of the Dean and Chapter of the cathedral church of Chichester 1472-1544* (1952) and *1545-1642* (1959)

Calendar of the Manuscripts of the Dean and Chapter of Wells (H.M.C., vol. I (1907) and II (1914))

Thompson, A Hamilton, *The English Clergy* (1947)

Williams, J F and **Cozens-Hardy, B,** *Extracts from the two earliest minute books of the Dean and Chapter of Norwich Cathedral* (1953)

Port Books

D M Woodward

[Entries from the Port Books of (i) the Southampton Searcher, 1565 (PRO.E190/814/1) and (ii) the Ipswich Controller, 1571-2 (PRO. E190/589/6).]

(i) xvi of auguste
In the marie of St vincent(es) of the burden of L tonnes m^r [i.e. ship's master]
    John penoya ffrom fflannderes to hampton
ffor the sam(e) mr [i.e. penoya] stranger in the said shippe thurtene tonnes of
ffrenche Irone
ffor m(ar)tine sause m(er)chant strannger tow tonnes of frenche Irone
    xxi die auguste
In the Clement of barckinge of the burden of x tonnes wherof Thomas hooll is m^r
ffreightid ffrom Roane to hampton
ffor Peter Stones of hampton m(er)chant englishe, eight milstones nynetene
ballet(es) towlas [i.e.Toulouse] woad waienge xxviii C(entum) di(midium)
one Casse & a half normandie glasse
    xxviii die auguste
In the ffortune of Torgooe [i.e. Tergul of the burden of xl tonnes wherof
Will(ia)me Johnssone is rrir ffreightid ffrom Norwaie to hampton
ffor the said m^r strangers threscore mastes, thurtie dowble Spares one hundred
    of dealle bordes one hundred & a half of sparres one hundred & a half of Rafteres.
(ii) Vicessimo tercio die Juiii
Le Marye Thomas de harwiche on(er)is lxx doll(eorum) m^r Will(ia)m Grene A
Irelond
Idem m^r de harwiche ind(igenus) on(er)avit unu(m)
    Laste Stockfyshe Croplinge vall(oris) — vi^{li} xiii^s iiii^d eodem} Subsi(dium)x^s
    p(ro) uno Laste Stockfyshe titfinge vall(oris) — iii^{li} vi^s viii^d }
Vis Viiid Vicesimo Quarto die Julii
Le harte de harwiche on(er)is vii dou(eorum) m^r will(ia)m charnell ib(ide)m A
Deipe
Thomas Aprise ind(igenus) on(er)at Quatuor centu(m)   }
    Libr(a) brasen vall(oris) — vi^{li} xiii^s iiii^d eodem p(ro)   } Subse(dium) viii^s
    uno cent(um) eflu packing canvas vall(oris) — xxvi^s vii^d }

The Port Books

The class of Exchequer, King's or Queen's Remembrancer, Port Books was established under an Exchequer Order of November 1564 in an attempt to tighten up the administration of the customs in England and Wales. Beginning at Easter 1565 blank Books were sent each year to the customs officers in all the ports and at the end of the year the officers were required to return their Books, containing details of the port's trade, to the Exchequer. Altogether nearly 20,000 Port Books have survived although some are in too dilapidated a condition to be consulted. It is clear, however, that the extant Books, which are kept at the Public Record Office in London, amount to only a small percentage of the total number of blank Books originally sent out from the Exchequer; some 4000 Books were issued for London during the period 1565 to 1697 but of these only 700 have survived. Except for considerable gaps in the series during the period of the Civil War and Interregnum the Port Books continued until the late eighteenth century when the series was ended by a Treasury Order of 14 March 1799. For some ports, however, Port Books are not available for the later eighteenth century; for example, the last Book for Poole covers the year 1759-60 while the last Book for Cardiff is for 1736. Unfortunately the London Books for 1697 to 1799 were destroyed in the 1890s because, it was argued, the series was incomplete and many of the existing Books were decayed or illegible.

Format

Port Books, with only a few exceptions, are made of parchment and range in size from thin Books of a few folios, which were sent to small ports such as Chichester or Bridlington, to the massive volumes for London which contain up to 700 folios. In the sixteenth century most of the Books were written in a kind of dog Latin peculiar to the customs house although some were already being written in English. During the seventeenth century more and more of the entries were made entirely in English and it is unusual to find a post-Restoration Book written in Latin. The transition to Arabic numerals was rather slower although examples of Port Books which contain few Roman numerals can be found for the sixteenth century.

Some of the Port Books contain details of both overseas and coasting trade but at most ports the details of these distinct branches of trade were recorded in separate Books. In making their entries the customs officers tended to follow a common pattern. They noted down the date and sometimes the time or tide, the name of the ship and also its port of provenance and burthen, the name of the ship's master and the ship's destination or port of sailing. This last detail, which was not always recorded, must be treated with caution; ships frequently traded with more than one port during a voyage and merchants sometimes gave false information to disguise the fact that they were infringing the rights of a monopoly trading company. Some officers, especially after the early seventeenth century, also failed to note down the ship's burthen. Following these entries the Books list the names of the merchants, and sometimes their home towns or whether or not they were English or aliens, and the cargoes they were shipping. Most Books finally noted down the values of the cargoes and the amount of duty paid. It should be noted that the valuations given in the Port Books were official values laid down in the Book of Rates, which was revised periodically, and not the real value of the goods. Sometimes the Books provide extra information such as merchants' marks reproduced in the margin, or, in the eighteenth century, whether or not the ship was British built. Details of provisions and munitions being sent for troops serving overseas are sometimes given and occasionally the Books record the movement of passengers; on I May 1699 the Controller of Portsmouth recorded the entry of 'a Danish Man of Warr from errance w(i)th trench Protestants'. (PRO. E190/841/5).

Like most manuscripts of the sixteenth and seventeenth centuries the Port

Books are sometimes difficult to read because of the vagaries of phonetic spelling. Foreign place names can be particularly difficult; for example, the 1576 London Port Book (PRO. E190/6/4) gives the following spellings for Ayamonte in southern Spain — Amonnte, Amonnty, Emonnte, Emonnty — and Konigsberg is rendered as Quenborough or variations of this. Most help with this problem can be obtained by reference to **Smit, H J**, *Bronnen Tot De Geschiedenis Van Den Handel met Engeland, Schotland en Ierland, 1485-1585* (2 vols The Hague, 1942 and 1950) and most difficulties with unusual commodities and their measures can be resolved by consulting *A Tudor Book of Rates* (see Bibliography). The names of the merchants, especially foreign merchants, can also provide difficulties and there are numerous abbreviations, such as hhd., ho., or hodgh. for hogshead, but these will soon be learned by experience.

The Uses of Port Books

The major use to which the Port Books can be put is in tracing the development of the trade of individual ports, groups of ports, regions, or the country as a whole. The Port Books can reveal, among other things, the changing geographical structure of trade, the growing or declining importance of particular commodities in the import and export trades, the proportion of trade conducted by British merchants or carried by British ships, the dominance of particular merchants over the trade of a port, and the efficacy of the control exercised over a particular branch of trade by a merchant company. It is also possible to suggest trends in the size of vessels being used, although here particular care must be taken. The tonnage data refer to the carrying capacity or burthen of the ships but is only a very rough indication of the size of the ship; the same ship is often accredited with a different burthen when it appears more than once in the same Book. When used in conjunction with local customs accounts, the ledgers, letter books, wills and probate inventories of local merchants, the records of trading companies and other material available in national and local archives it is possible to build up a well-rounded picture of the trade and mercantile community of particular areas. The Port Books can also be useful to historians whose primary concern is not with the development of trade. Thus the historian of industrial development can trace the import of raw materials and the export of finished goods, while the historian of a port's social structure will be able to discover the size of the active merchant community and the names of individual merchants, both great and small.

Many historians have pointed out that the Port Books under-recorded the volume of trade because of two types of fraudulent activity; smuggling and the deliberate failure of the officers to record some cargoes in order to augment their somewhat meagre stipends by pocketing the duty paid to them by the merchants. Thus it is clear that the Port Books do not provide trade 'statistics' but only a record of a part of the trade passing through particular ports. Instances of large scale smuggling and corruption are not too difficult to find, but this should not lead historians to condemn all Port Books out of hand. The

Port Books

volume of smuggling varied from time to time, the problem becoming particularly acute in the eighteenth century, and also from port to port. Some ports were more favourably situated for illicit trade and it can be assumed that the vigour and honesty of the customs officers also varied.

Thus, users of the Port Books must always be on their guard against the seemingly comprehensive nature of the data provided. They must attempt to assess the reliability of the Books consulted by searching for the records of inquiries into fraudulent activity and by checking the Books against local customs accounts, where these exist. It may also be possible to check detailed entries in the Port Books against entries in merchants' ledgers and it is always interesting to discover what merchants thought about the state of trade at a particular time; confidence in the Port Books is increased if the trends of the trade they record correspond with what merchants were saying about their fortunes. Port Books may not provide an accurate series of data, but without them it would be extremely difficult, and often impossible, to make any meaningful statement about the development of trade, especially in the sixteenth and seventeenth centuries.

Bibliography

There are useful introductions in:

Hinton, R W K (ed), *The Port Books of Boston, 1600-1640* (Lincoln Record Society, vol. 50, 1956)

Lewis, E A (ed), *The Welsh Port Books, 1550-1603* (Cymmrodorion Record Series No. XII, 1927)

Williams, N J (ed), *Descriptive List of Exchequer, Queen's Remembrancer, Port Books, Part 1, 1565 to 1700* (PRO., London 1960). A list for subsequent years is in the PRO., to be published by the List and Index Society.

Further background information is given in:

Andrews, J H, 'Two Problems in the Interpretations of the Port Books' *Economic History Review* (2nd series, Vol. IX, 1956)

Clark, G N, *Guide to English Commercial Statistics, 1696-1782* (London 1938)

Jarvis, R C, 'Sources for the History of Ports', *Journal of Transport History* (Vol. 3, 1957-8)

Stephens, W B, 'The Exchequer Port Books as a Source for the History of the English Cloth Trade', *Textile History*, i. (1969), 206-13

Willan, T S, *The English Coasting Trade,1600-1750* (Manchester, 1938)

Willan, T S (ed), *A Tudor Book of Rates* (Manchester, 1962)

Quarter Sessions Order Books

Richard Hunt

[Extract from B C Redwood, Quarter Sessions Order Book 1642-1649. Sussex Record Society, vol. 54 (1954) p. 168]. 1649.

Cosely bridge Whereas the Inhabitants of the hamlett of Withiham doe stand indicted for there default in not repayring Cosely bridge and John Baker one of the Inhabitants of the sayd hamlett is returned by the Sheriff in the name of the rest of the sayd Inhabitants and is assigned to repayre the sayd bridge before the feast of St John Baptist next and to certify thereof at the next Sessions following It is ordered that a Tax shalbe made by the Inhabitants of the sayd hamlett as wen for the charges which shalbe layd out in repayring the sayd bridge as also for the Costs charges and expences in discharging the Indictment and otherwise occasioned hereby And if any refuse to pay they shalbe bound over to the next Sessions to answer their Contempt.

[Extract from East Sussex County Record Office (QO/EW20 1750-1756), 1750]

Alverstoke & Bosham Order for remove of James Hatfield & his wife continued. — Upon the Appeal of the Parishioners of the Parish of Alverstoke in the County of Southampton from an Order or Warrant of two of his Majesty's Justices of the Peace of the said County of Sussex for removing of James Hatfield and Sarah his wife from the Parish of Bosham in the said County of Sussex to the said Parish of Alverstoke And upon hearing of Council on both sides It is ordered by this Court that the said Order or Warrant of the said two Justices of the Peace be confirmed and by this Court it is Confirmed accordingly.

Treas. to pay Willm— Bell 0^l 12^s 4^d — It is ordered by this Court that M' William White Treasurer of the Tax made for conveying of vagrants and other Uses within the Best Part of the said County do immediately upon sight hereof pay unto William Bell one of the Constables of the Borough of Midhurst the sum of Twelve Shillings and Four Pence for conveying of vagrants by Order of the Justices.

Quarter Sessions

Quarter Sessions were the meetings of the Justices of the Peace for each county held at Easter, Trinity, Michaelmas and Epiphany to deal with cases, both judicial and administrative, that they were empowered to hear and determine under the law. The court occupied an intermediate position in local government between that of individual J.P.s, or groups of two or three justices, hearing cases out of Sessions (which developed into petty sessions in the late seventeenth and eighteenth centuries) and the Assizes, where the gravest offences and the more complex or contentious disputes were heard. The J.P.s were local amateurs, the Assize Judges royal judges of the central courts coming round on circuit. The quarterly meetings of Justices of the Peace started in the fourteenth century. During the Tudor period the sphere of their activities was increased by the central government to enforce the growing

Short Guides to Records 23

number of statutes which sought to regulate so many aspects of the economic and social life of the country. The Quarter Sessions of the counties and of the corporate towns gradually replaced the Sheriff as the main organ of local government. It was not until the Municipal Corporations Act of 1835 and the Local Government Act of 1888 that administrative control, of towns and counties respectively, passed from the hands of the Justices, although the advent of a number of ad hoc bodies in the nineteenth century, such as the Boards of Poor Law Guardians after 1834, meant that the scope of the Justices' activities was gradually reduced. Prior to the nineteenth-century reforms there was no clear distinction between the judicial and administrative functions of Quarter Sessions. The legal process was usually of a judicial form, whereby individuals, groups or even the entire inhabitants of a parish might be presented and indicted for failure to comply with a regulation or a previous Order of the court.

Order Books

It may be useful to outline the relationship of Sessions Order Books to the other classes of Sessions records. Sessions Rolls or Files, if well kept, contain all the original documents used at a session. The largest and most formal document in the Sessions Rolls is the calendar, usually giving names of all justices in the commission, with dots against those actually present. Where this is not available students will have to turn to the Pipe Rolls (PRO E/372) where the sheriff named the justices sitting when claiming their payment from the Exchequer. Indictment or Process Books give very brief particulars of defendant, offence, plea, verdict and, occasionally, sentence (purely judicial business often excluded from the Order Books). Minute or Sessions Books contain rough notes on all the business of the court of Quarter Sessions. The Order Books are the formal record of the court, containing carefully entered copies of the Justices' Orders, usually with more detail than the Minute Books, and more useful explanation of cases. The Order Books may, however, provide interesting references to cases dealt with by Justices 'out of Sessions' — the only guide we have, apart from some very rare private note books, of this sphere of the work done by Justices. One of the reasons for the compilation of the formal record was to aid Justices and the Clerk of the Peace with cases still in hand, but Order Books were also used as precedent books for future judgements and, in addition to Orders, they may contain reports from individual Justices, committees and county officials, with the subsequent Order from Sessions, and occasionally precedents or recommendations from the Assize judges. Many Order Books have useful contemporary indexes and, although they lack some of the interesting detail to be found in the Rolls or Files and present only a part of the picture of the activities of the Justices in Sessions, they are the most convenient and accessible of Quarter Sessions records.

Location

The records of Quarter Sessions are in the custody of the Clerk of the Peace, and are to be found in the County Record Office. It is broadly true to say that Record Offices were originally established to preserve and catalogue the Quarter Sessions records and other records of the Clerk of the Peace. These were formerly in the custody of the Custos Rotulorum who frequently deputed the task to the Clerk of the Peace. Until recent times the Clerk was usually an attorney in private practice and the wide variation in the survival of the records is attributable to the different practices of Clerks. Some records were passed on to successors in office, others were deposited in private archives, while yet others must have been lost or destroyed. The earliest Order Books are those for Wiltshire for which some records for 1563 are extant and a series starts in 1575. The earliest in Devon are of 1592, but for most of England Order Books start in the seventeenth century. Bedford, Berkshire, Cornwall, Huntingdon, Peterborough (Soke), Rutland and the Welsh counties, with the exceptions of Brecon (1679) and Caernarvon (1633), start in the eighteenth century. *County Records* (bibliography) outlines the availability of Order Books and some other classes of County records.

The Uses of Sessions Order Books

Order Books offer interesting and valuable material for the local historian of either county or parish. They are an important primary source for the history of those administrative, social and economic activities with which Quarter Sessions were concerned. As the illustrations show, Orders are entered in the Books in the order of the court hearings and are not arranged by subject or parish. The only immediate point of reference is the date of the Sessions, but the marginal index often gives the names of persons and parishes which are the subject of the Order. The parish historian can quite easily trace entries relating to his parish and, because of the custom of identifying persons by their parish of settlement in legal records, entries relating to individuals from the parish. The other common convention of giving the occupation or status of persons provides additionally useful material. Order Books only incidentally name parish officials and are therefore of limited value in identifying constables, overseers and churchwardens.

Perhaps the main value of the Order Books is in helping with an analysis of the various aspects of government which came under the control of Justices of the Peace. The range of these aspects is so large that they can only be outlined here under broad headings. All aspects of judicial proceedings under the criminal law, often including preliminary hearings of cases that went to Assizes; religious matters such as recusancy and conventicles; general administrative matters such as taxation and rating; the Poor Law and vagrancy (which certainly occupy the greatest volume in the records); highways and bridges; licensing and the control of markets; all these were partially or wholly controlled by Justices, and the Orders itemise their decisions taken while exercising their highest authority. In addition there are occasional references to special contingencies such as outbreaks of disease or fire, and to events of national importance, usually in relation to communications from Whitehall. Letters from the Privy Council are often mentioned in Order Books, especially in the seventeenth century, and the original letters are often preserved in the

Quarter Sessions Order Books

Sessions Rolls, though these will not be as complete as the Privy Council registers.

In attempting to analyse the material to be found in Order Books perhaps the most useful method is by comparison of particular aspects, either by area (parish or hundred within the county, or county against county) or period. The former comparison can highlight the difference in the incidence of particular infringements between different kinds of communities — scattered or nucleated populations perhaps. The latter can pinpoint years or periods when the attention of the Justices was concentrated on select aspects of law enforcement, or show trends of increase or decrease in the incidence of infringements within a single community.

Like all legal records, Order Books suffer from the limitation that Orders were usually made on the infringement of a regulation or in the event of a dispute. They therefore offer little evidence of the normal state of affairs, with rates being collected or the poor relieved without complaint. Nevertheless the Orders remain the best guide to the history of county government, and their value can be considerably enhanced if they are studied in conjunction with other classes of documents. These include (1) the other Quarter Sessions records mentioned above; (2) parish records, such as constables and churchwardens' accounts, or vestry minutes; (3) central government records especially Privy Council Registers (PC/2), which contain circular letters of direction to Sessions (as well as Lord and Deputy Lieutenants) and occasional specific directions to particular county Sessions; Assize records, which are few and far between before the early nineteenth century; and the Pipe Rolls mentioned above.

Bibliography

Barnes, T G, *Somerset, 1625-40* (1961)

Dowdell, E G, *One Hundred Years of Quarter Sessions* (1932). Based on Middlesex Sessions 1660-1760

Emmison, F G and **Gray, Irvine**, *County Records* Historical Association (1961)

Johnson, H C, 'The Origin and Office of the Clerk of the Peace', in *The Clerks of the Counties* edited by Sir Edgar Stephens (1961)

Moir, Esther, *The Justice of the Peace* (1969)

Peyton, S A (ed), *Minutes of Proceedings in Quarter Sessions* (Lincoln Record Society, vol. 25 (1931)), which has a very useful introduction

Webb, S and **B**, *English Local Government: the Parish and the County* (1906)

The following counties have catalogues or transcripts of some county records printed either by the local record society or the county council: Bedfordshire, Berkshire, Buckinghamshire, Caernarvonshire, Cheshire, Derbyshire, Dorset, Essex, Flintshire, Gloucestershire, Hertfordshire, Kent, Lancashire, Lincolnshire, Middlesex, Northamptonshire, Nottinghamshire, Oxfordshire, Shropshire, Somerset (also some seventeenth-century Assize records), Staffordshire, Surrey, Sussex, Warwickshire, Wiltshire, Worcestershire, Yorkshire (North and West Ridings).

Local Reports to the General Board of Health

H J Smith

[Extracts from G T Clark, Report ... on a preliminary inquiry into ... the sanitary condition of the inhabitants of the parish and town of Pool or Welshpool (London, 1850); and W Lee, Report ... the parish of Longbridge Deverill (London, 1852)]

(Welshpool) My Lords and Gentlemen, In obedience to your instructions I have inspected the parish and town of Pool ... After notice duly given I held public sittings in the Town-hall there on the 9th, 10th and 11th instant, and employed the remainder of those days in inspecting the place, and in collecting the materials for the report which I have now the honour to lay before you.

2. This Report, although addressed to the General Board, is to be published in the district of Pool, and may be officially commented upon by the rate-payers, for which reason I have introduced some topics and explained others, in a manner which would have been uncalled for had the report been intended for the General Board only.

....

(Longbridge Deverill) Minutes of My Inspection

Eli Tooze, living in the next house, said:- 'We have had five children, but they are all dead. I have always lived in this parish. I had the ague first when I was ten years of age; four years ago I was ill of it twenty five weeks; I am ill now, and shall never be well again. My wife is unfit to do anything, she is so ill. She has not been well for some years, and has had the chill.'

Unable to stand, this poor woman was sitting in a chair, endeavouring to wash a few clothes in some very dirty water. Both husband and wife looked more than half dead. The tears ran down both their faces while telling me their sorrowful tale.

....

(Welshpool) REMEDIES

86. The application of the Public Health Act to Welsh-Pool will, in the first place, and as a basis to all future improvements, at once, within its own province, remove all the anomalies and complexities of the present local government ... The direct penny's worth will be sensibly received by each person who pays the penny.

Origin and Format

Two influences have to be distinguished in the making of these reports. Firstly, epidemic dangers and insanitary conditions in the towns led to the passing of the Public Health Act (1 1 & 12 Vict. cap. 63) in 1848. The General Board of Health was set up with powers to inquire into localities petitioning for application of the act; or to initiate such inquiries where mortality exceeded 23 in 1,000. Inspectors were sent to conduct these inquiries and their reports form the subject of this guide. If they recommended application of the act, local boards of health were created.

But a second influence was the need of a cheap, uniform and expeditious method of inquiry into local government; and to achieve its reform. The enormous costs of private acts of improvement had already led to the Act for

Local Reports to the General Board of Health
Preliminary Inquiries (9 & 10 Vict. cap. 106, amended by 11 & 12 Vict. cap. 129) authorising the Commissioners of Woods and Forests and the Board of Admiralty to carry them out. A select committee of 1850 found there had been no gains in time or economy, while in this period the machinery of the Public Health Act was meeting the problem. Although for the specific purpose of sanitary reform, the General Board's inquiries inevitably exposed inadequacies of local government and dwelt on this aspect: Birmingham with its eight separate governing bodies — similarly Bristol, Portsmouth and Macclesfield; Nantwich had only manorial government; Llanelly the improvisations of a chamber of commerce; Swindon relied on parochial administration, and Newton Abbot formed 'no exception to the mass of small towns possessing only a village government'. Applications for Public Health inquiries were in many cases inspired by the desire to reform or acquire a local administration as at Bryn Mawr, Sherbourne, Burley and St. Helen's. The report on Over Darwen asserted, 'The principle of consolidation in local government is one which pervades the Public Health Act from beginning to end . . .'; that for Bridgend declared, 'The one grand remedial measure, without which nothing can be economically or efficiently executed for the general improvement of the town, is a responsible local government . . .'

The reports are of two kinds; the most important and the majority are the preliminary inquiries which cover all aspects of the locality's sanitary condition. The other are the further inquiries made necessary because the creation of a local board involved alteration of existing boundaries; or concern graveyards, drainage schemes and the conduct of existing boards. This guide refers chiefly to the reports of preliminary inquiries.

Printed in octavo, varying between the 224 pages for Bristol and the 12 pages for Alvaston and Boulton, the reports were intended for local circulation as well as for the information of the General Board of Health. They were meant to be 'practically useful'; as the Much Woolton report says,

... each report is new to the particular locality to which it refers, and one object alone is sought through the publication of all the Reports, namely, to point out the actual condition of each district, to set forth prominently those evils which may be removed, and briefly to inculcate the advantages of applying an efficient remedy.

Thus besides evidence, correspondence and statistics, they frequently specify measures to be taken, offer cost estimates, and answer popular misconceptions about the Public Health Act, the General Board and powers of local boards. The contents of the Portsmouth report include the correspondence leading to the inquiry, the early history of the town, details of local acts of Parliament, rating lists, population and mortality figures, the history of the town's water supply, slaughter house regulation; and close with the inspector's formal recommendations. Two appendices give the evidence of house to house inspection and discuss the problems of deep drainage. The Shrewsbury report tidily divides 20 pages of general statements from 105 pages of statistics and evidence. The Southampton report gives meteorological information; discusses the moral causes of disease; names the unsewered streets and ways; describes privy accommodation in working class districts, the numbers of street lamps and the distance between them (having a bearing on public morality), head-stone fees, the funeral expenses of a late deceased gentleman, arrestable offences in 1849, the expenses of cultivating a quarter-acre, and dame schools. The Whitehaven report has 15 very detailed pages concerning the occupants, furniture and ventilation of tenements. The majority of reports are accompanied with well defined maps: the spirit vaults, gas lamps, privies and pig-sties of Hexham are marked on a scale of 100 feet to the inch. A map in the Norwich report uniquely charts river pollution. Plans and sections are plentiful; in a minority of reports scenic illustrations occur. But variations in amount and type of evidence are many, and show the extent to which the reports relied not only on the findings of the inspector but on the collaboration and contributions of interested persons and public authorities locally.

Uses of the Reports

The uses of these reports are manifold for they include every topic which in the opinion of the inspector affected the moral and physical welfare, and the government of the locality he visited. Every kind of statistic appears, in one report or another, to have been grist to the mill; and so a highly detailed and often dramatic picture of the community as it was in the period 1848-57 emerges. Since the reports have this rather general usefulness it is as well to say what proportion of the country they covered. With London excepted from the authority of the General Board of Health, 3.6 million of the inhabitants of England and Wales lived in places reported upon, or approximately 23% of the total population outside London in 1851. The proportions vary between a total of 48 counties: at one end of the scale, Warwickshire 66%, Glamorgan 58%, Staffordshire 51%, Gloucestershire (with Bristol) 46%, Durham 38%; at the other, Northamptonshire and Oxfordshire 5%, and Pembrokeshire 3%. In between we find Middlesex 25%, Yorkshire 22%, Lancashire 14% and Cheshire 13%. Of 62 towns with over 20,000 inhabitants, 36 were visited and the new suburbs of five others. Thirty-three places with a population under 2000 were also reported upon. The localities differ markedly in type: the well-to-do suburbs of Manchester at Broughton, Rusholme and Mosside seeking amenities and powers of government; likewise Poulton Bare and Torrisholme, a fashionable sea-bathing town in construction; the almost exclusively proletarian Merthyr Tydfil and Dukinfield; the 'delightful village' of Southborough; and Macclesfield 'ranking among the worst known in the empire' for sanitary conditions.

The reports reveal the public reception of a significant and controversial piece of nineteenth century reform legislation. The inspectors impress the reader not only with their thoroughness and expedition, but also with the attention they paid to cultivating opinion and answering opposition: evening sittings of the inquiry to allow working-class people to attend; open-air sittings at Merthyr Tydfil before some 6 to 900 people with simultaneous translation of the proceedings into Welsh. The inspectors almost always refer to, and sometimes identify the support and the opposition they met with: at Newton Heath miraculous support indeed as the noisy opponents of improved drainage were quelled by a sudden eclipse of the sun and a very heavy rainfall which resulted in the providential flooding of their homes.

Location

It appears that 398 reports were published between 1848 and 1857. They refer to 296 localities and include the further inquiries which were necessary in some cases. The most complete collection is that in the library of the Department of Health and Social Services at Alexander Fleming House: 395 reports for 296 localities. The British Museum collection, better known, was not acquired under the copyright privilege but from the estate of Sir Edwin Chadwick in 1891. This consists of 375 reports for 279 localities. There are no other collections of this completeness. The only other sizeable collections are at Sheffield University (39 reports), Birmingham Public Library (25), Cardiff Public Library (I 5), Manchester Public Library (I 2) and London University (8). Two libraries have 5 each; Leicester City Library has four including one report not in either of the two London collections. Nowhere outside London is there a full collection for any one county. Of course, local newspapers very frequently reproduced the reports in their entirety at the time of publication. Photo-copies can be obtained from the British Museum and the Department of Health and Social Security, the latter being ready to loan its loose copies for this purpose. The British Museum Catalogue should be consulted for the localities reported on. It does not include the following: preliminary inquiries at Aldershot, Arnold, Basingstoke, Brentwood, Bridgnorth, Caverswall, Crumpsall, Cwmdu, Droitwich, Hexham, Milton next Sittingbourne, Seaford, Skipton, Thornton, Upton cum Chalvey, and Ynyscynhaiarn; further inquiries at Caverswall, Dalton, Haworth and Skipton; third reports on Leicester and Newton Heath.

Bibliography

British Museum, *General Catalogue of Printed Books* v. LXIV (1961) cols. 2194-2237

Lewis, R A, *Edwin Chadwick & the Public Health Movement* (London, 1952), chap. xiii, 'The inspectors at work'

Parliamentary Papers, 1849, XXIV, pp. 129-35 and 1854, vol. XXXV, pp. 96-102, for 'Instructions ... to the superintending inspectors'. Ibid., 1852-53, vol. XCVI, for 'Returns of all places which have petitioned ... for the application of the Public Health Act ...' **Of the reports themselves, the following may be consulted for what they reveal of their background and preparation: Reading, King's Lynn, Great Crosby & Litherland, and Report on a Memorial from Great Yarmouth.**

Smith, H J, intro., **Ranger, W,** *Report ... sanitary condition of ... Darlington* (Durham Local History Society, 1967) for a recently republished example